CAMBRIDGE LIBRARY COLLECTION

Books of enduring scholarly value

Polar Exploration

This series includes accounts, by eye-witnesses and contemporaries, of early expeditions to the Arctic and the Antarctic. Huge resources were invested in such endeavours, particularly the search for the North-West Passage, which, if successful, promised enormous strategic and commercial rewards. Cartographers and scientists travelled with many of the expeditions, and their work made important contributions to earth sciences, climatology, botany and zoology. They also brought back anthropological information about the indigenous peoples of the Arctic region and the southern fringes of the American continent. The series further includes dramatic and poignant accounts of the harsh realities of working in extreme conditions and utter isolation in bygone centuries.

Cruise of the *Pandora*

Sir Allen Young (1827–1915), merchant navy officer and experienced Polar explorer, took part in several expeditions before that of the *Pandora*. As navigator he had accompanied the McClintock expedition to discover the fate of Sir John Franklin, during which he explored several hundred miles of new coastline by sledge. He was also in command of the *Fox* on the 1860 North Atlantic telegraph expedition to assess the practicality of a cable route between Europe and America across the Faroes, Iceland and Greenland. In 1875, he led, and financed, the British North-West Passage Expedition on the *Pandora*, and this compelling account of his journey was first published in 1876. In it, he records his attempt to reach the magnetic pole via Baffin Bay and Lancaster Sound, and to navigate the North-West Passage in one season, though he failed in this attempt because of heavy ice in the Franklin Strait.

T0345436

Cambridge University Press has long been a pioneer in the reissuing of out-of-print titles from its own backlist, producing digital reprints of books that are still sought after by scholars and students but could not be reprinted economically using traditional technology. The Cambridge Library Collection extends this activity to a wider range of books which are still of importance to researchers and professionals, either for the source material they contain, or as landmarks in the history of their academic discipline.

Drawing from the world-renowned collections in the Cambridge University Library and other partner libraries, and guided by the advice of experts in each subject area, Cambridge University Press is using state-of-the-art scanning machines in its own Printing House to capture the content of each book selected for inclusion. The files are processed to give a consistently clear, crisp image, and the books finished to the high quality standard for which the Press is recognised around the world. The latest print-on-demand technology ensures that the books will remain available indefinitely, and that orders for single or multiple copies can quickly be supplied.

The Cambridge Library Collection brings back to life books of enduring scholarly value (including out-of-copyright works originally issued by other publishers) across a wide range of disciplines in the humanities and social sciences and in science and technology.

Cruise of the *Pandora*

*From the Private Journal
Kept by Allen Young
Commander of the Expedition*

ALLEN YOUNG

CAMBRIDGE
UNIVERSITY PRESS

CAMBRIDGE UNIVERSITY PRESS

Cambridge, New York, Melbourne, Madrid, Cape Town,
Singapore, São Paolo, Delhi, Mexico City

Published in the United States of America by Cambridge University Press, New York

www.cambridge.org
Information on this title: www.cambridge.org/9781108049733

© in this compilation Cambridge University Press 2012

This edition first published 1876
This digitally printed version 2012

ISBN 978-1-108-04973-3 Paperback

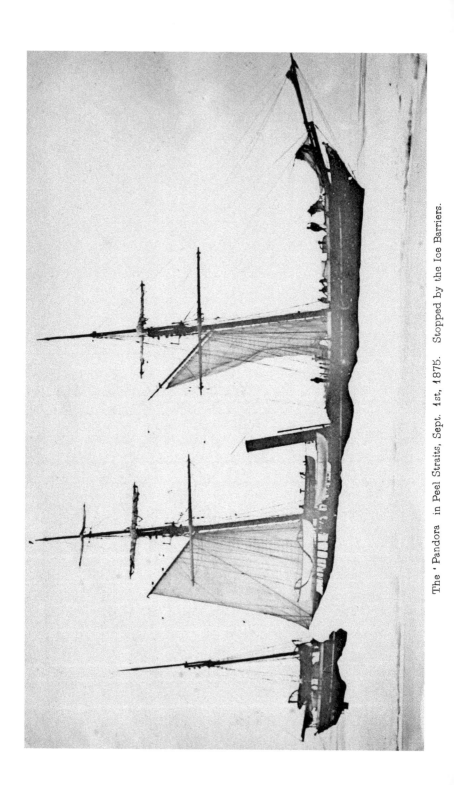

The 'Pandora' in Peel Straits, Sept. 1st, 1875. Stopped by the Ice Barriers.

CRUISE OF THE 'PANDORA.'

FROM

THE PRIVATE JOURNAL

KEPT BY

ALLEN YOUNG, R.N.R., F.R.G.S., F.R.A.S., &c.,

COMMANDER OF THE EXPEDITION,

1876.

LONDON: PRINTED BY WILLIAM CLOWES AND SONS, STAMFORD STREET AND CHARING CROSS.

INTRODUCTION.

THIS narrative has been printed in order that there may be an authentic record of the voyage of the R.Y.S. steam yacht 'Pandora' to the Arctic Seas, in 1875.

The objects of the voyage were to visit the western coast of Greenland, thence to proceed through Baffin's Sea, Lancaster Sound, and Barrow Strait, towards the magnetic pole, and, if practicable, to navigate through the North-West Passage to the Pacific Ocean in one season. As, in following this route, the 'Pandora' would pass King William's Island, it was proposed, if successful in reaching that locality, in the summer season, when the snow was off the land, to make a search for further records and for the journals of the ships 'Erebus' and 'Terror,' which were both lost in attempting the same voyage.

As no possible advantage to this project could be gained by wintering, it was arranged that the great loss of time and additional expense attending a ten months' purposeless detention in the Arctic Seas should be avoided, if possible, unless such a position could be attained as would render it advisable. In the event of the latter contingency, the 'Pandora' was fully equipped, and the crew were engaged to remain for a period of two years' absence from home.

The 'Pandora' was formerly a despatch gun-vessel, and was purchased from the Admiralty. She was built for speed, under sail or steam, or both combined, and fitted with engines of 80 horse-power. The ship was taken to the works of Messrs. Day and Summers, at Southampton, to be fortified and prepared with all the modern equipments of an Arctic exploring ship. She was rigged as a barquentine, and carried eight boats, including a steam cutter and three whale-boats.

When the repairs and alterations were completed, the 'Pandora' was removed to the docks, and provisioned and stored for eighteen months. The officers and crew were selected, and she anchored in the Southampton Water in June, to receive her gunpowder, and to make final preparations for her adventurous cruise.

The 'Pandora' carried the white ensign and burgee of the Royal Yacht Squadron, and her complement of officers and men was thirty-one all told, as follows :

1. *Captain.*—ALLEN YOUNG,[1] R.N.R.
2. *Lieutenant.*—F. INNES LILLINGSTON,[2] R.N.
3.   „   GEORGE PIRIE,[3] R.N.
4.   „   KOOLEMANS BEYNAN,[4] R.N.N.

---

[1] Captain Allen Young entered the merchant service in 1846. He commanded the 'Marlborough,' East Indiaman, 1500 tons, twice round the world, 1853–54; and the 'Adelaide,' steam troop-ship, 3000 tons, during the Crimean war, 1855–56. He was sailing-master of the 'Fox' (M'Clintock), 1857–59, and commenced his tarvelling work by laying out a depôt between February 15 and March 3, the thermometer averaging − 40 to − 48; mercury frozen all the time. On his return he started for Fury Beach to get some stores left by Parry, absent from March 18 to 28. He started again on April 7, tracing the south and west shores of Prince of Wales' Land. After thirty-eight days he sent back the men and tent, owing to provisions running short, and went on for forty days with one man and the dogs, sleeping each night in a hole in the snow. He attempted to cross the M'Clintock Channel, and went about forty miles from the land, the ice being frightfully heavy. He reached the ship on June 7, after an absence of seventy-eight days. He went again to explore Peel Sound from June 10 to 28. He then connected Osborn's with Browne's furthest, and discovered 380 miles of new coast line. He became a Lieutenant of the Naval Reserve, February 24, 1862. F.R.G.S. and F.R.A.S. He commanded the 'Fox' in the North Atlantic Telegraph Expedition in 1862, going to Faroe Isles, Iceland, and Greenland, and the 'Quantung,' in the European Chinese Navy, 1862–64. He was Commissioner to the Maritime Congress at Naples in 1871.

Author of an account of the voyage of the 'Fox,' in the first number of the 'Cornhill Magazine;' republished in 1875 by Mr. Griffin, of Portsea.

[2] Lieutenant in the Royal Navy, on the retired list, September 7, 1871.

[3] Navigating Sub-Lieutenant in the Royal Navy, on the active list, July 27, 1870.

[4] Lieutenant in the Royal Dutch Navy, and had served in the Sumatra Squadron, and on shore in the naval brigade at Achín. He is now engaged in editing a second edition of the 'Voyages of Barents to the North-East,' for the Hakluyt Society.

5. *Surgeon and Naturalist.*—Arthur Horner.
6. *Artist.*—Mr. De Wilde.
7. *Correspondent.*—J. A. MacGahan.
8. *First Engineer.*—Benjamin Ball.
9. *Second Engineer.*—Archibald Porteous.
10. *Gunner.*—Harry Toms.[1]
11. *Carpenter.*—Robert James.
12. *Boatswain.*—Henry Mitchell.
13. *Sailmaker.*—John Mott.
14. *Ship's Steward.*—William Edwards.
15. *Ward-room Steward.*—Joseph Lawrence.
16. *Captain of Hold.*—Thomas Florance.[2]
17. *Cook.*—Joseph Shelton.
18. *Interpreter.*—Eskimo Joe.
19. *Quartermaster.*—Henry Andrews.
20.   „   William Randerson.
21.   „   James Timpson.
22.   „   Henry Mihill.
23. *Captain's Coxswain.*—Charles Vine.
24. *Boatswain's Mate.*—Charles Tizzard.
25. *Harpooneer.*—Allan Gillies.
26. *Able Seaman.*—Edward Grace.
27.   „   William Davis.
28.   „   James Pennington.
29.   „   G. W. Thorne.
30. *Blacksmith and Stoker.*—Edwin Griffey.
31. *Stoker.*—James Cole.

The expenses of the expedition, and the purchase and equipment of the 'Pandora,' were undertaken by myself; and I was assisted by contributions from the late Lady Franklin, who never ceased to take the greatest interest in Arctic matters; from Mr. James Gordon Bennett, who was desirous of sending a correspondent; and from Lieutenant Lillingston, who accompanied me as second in command.

---

[1] Mr. Toms was a Quartermaster in the 'Fox,' with Sir Leopold M'Clintock, during her memorable voyage in 1857–59.

[2] Thomas Florance served in the 'North Star,' under Captain Pullen, 1852–54, and also in the 'Fox,' with Sir Leopold M'Clintock, as stoker.

ILLUSTRATIONS.

———◆◇◆———

CONTENTS.

———◆◆———

CHAPTER IX.

CHAPTER X.

CHAPTER XI.

CHAPTER XII.

CHAPTER XIII.

APPENDIX.

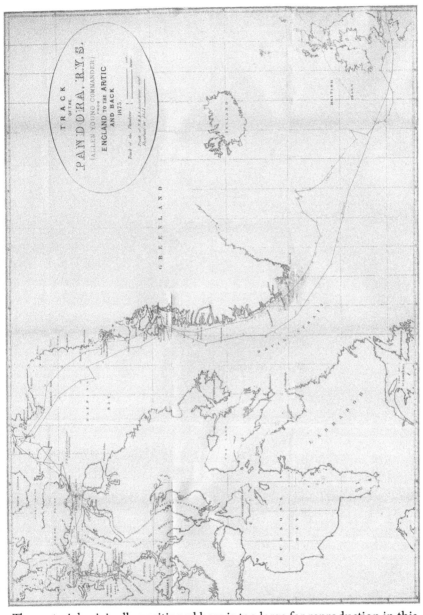

The material originally positioned here is too large for reproduction in this reissue. A PDF can be downloaded from the web address given on page iv of this book, by clicking on 'Resources Available'.

CRUISE OF THE 'PANDORA.

CHAPTER I.

THE VOYAGE TO GREENLAND.

ON the 25th of June, everything being reported ready for
sea, we slipped from the buoy off the Southampton Pier, and
proceeded round to Portsmouth. We had already received
on board two bags of letters for the 'Alert' and 'Discovery,'
besides parcels, which had been forwarded in the hope of our
being able to deliver them, or deposit them at the entrance of
Smith Sound. On entering Portsmouth Harbour, a message
was received from the Admiral to the effect that we might
go alongside the dockyard, and we accordingly moored by
the Queen's Steps at 9 P.M. I was much touched by the
hearty sympathy which I received at Portsmouth. I had
endeavoured, from the commencement, to keep our cruise
quite unnoticed, and had carefully avoided all demonstra-
tions; but, as we passed out of Portsmouth harbour, the
crews of all Her Majesty's ships gave us hearty cheers, to
which we responded in the best manner we could with our
little crew, and by dipping our colours.

We arrived at Cowes in the evening of June 26th, where
I had to meet Mr. Harper, our agent, who came to examine
the accounts with me, and to make final arrangements for
the pay of the crew, and for the payment of allotments to
their wives and families.

Having taken farewell of my friends at Cowes, I embarked

at midnight, intending to sail for Plymouth on the first of the ebb next morning. Accordingly, on June 27, we slipped from the buoy at 4 A.M. It was a lovely morning, with scarcely a breath of wind, as we passed out through the Needles, and proceeded with all fore and aft canvas. As we passed Portland, H.M.S. 'Warrior' signalled, "Wish you all success;" and, in answer, we signalled our thanks. Passing close round the Bill, we caught a fair wind from the southward, and made all sail, letting the steam run down.

I was pleased with the performance of the ship under canvas. She made a good six knots with the screw down. We saw the Start at 9 P.M., and it began to blow and rain in torrents, the wind being S.S.W. So we struck all canvas, and steamed again, arriving at Plymouth at 9 A.M., when I immediately sent on shore for 10 tons of coal, and also asked Lieut. Lillingston to call upon Admiral Sir H. Keppel, and to express my regret that I was unable to come personally. By the time we had completed our coaling, Admiral Keppel and Earl Mount Edgcumbe most kindly came on board to greet us, and to say good-bye. At six o'clock we steamed out. When off the Eddystone we made all plain sail and stopped the engines, steering off to S.W. with a light N.W. breeze, and, having set the watch, we all turned in. At noon, on the 29th, we passed the Lizard, and at 1.20 sent letters on board the ship 'Queen of Australia,' from Calcutta, bound for Dundee.

After July 18, we experienced nothing but alternate west winds and calms, with generally a high swell from the westward. We continued beating to windward, taking advantage of everything in our favour; but we made but slow progress, owing to our being so deep, and the ship's bottom so foul with grass from lying in the Southampton Water. On the 19th, we were in lat. 58° 58′ N., long. 31° 33′ W. I had endeavoured to get to the northward, in hopes of some change in the weather, which seemed so unusual for this season, and so opposite to our experience when crossing in the 'Fox.'

We constantly saw finner whales (*Physalus antiquorum* [1]) generally going to the northward. Since the 12th, we had been accompanied by mullemokkes (*Fulmar petrels*),[2] and since the 16th by a number of shearwaters (*Puffinus Anglorum* [3]), which we passed in flocks on the water. We had calms on the 23rd, 24th, and 25th, with light winds from N. and N.E., followed by a fresh N.W. to W. wind on the 26th, when we were in lat. 57° 55', long. 42° 49', Cape Farewell being N. 17, W. 119 miles. On the 27th, I went on board the 'Traveller,' of Peterhead, and obtained newspapers, and proceeded in company with her on the 28th, on which day we saw the first icebergs. The next morning we had a fresh breeze from the E.S.E., and at 5 saw the first Spitzbergen ice. We passed a few straggling pieces, and at 6 P.M. came upon several streams of ice. I then kept away to the westward, but finding that the wind was increasing, and a thick fog coming on to seaward, I steered in to the N.E. to go on through the ice, and to get into the land water. At noon, we were in lat. 60° 14' N., long. 68° 20' W., the land about Cape Desolation being plainly in sight whenever it cleared. Throughout the afternoon we were sailing through heavy ice, and received some severe blows; but towards evening, as we hauled into the

---

[1] *Physalus antiquorum* of Gray (or *Balænoptera musculus*) is the big finner, rorqual, or razor back, a cetacean from 60 to 70 feet long, black above and white below, with the flippers black. The old name given by Fabricius is *Balæna physalus*. The Eskimo name is *Tunnolik*. It is not seen farther north than Rifkol.

[2] The *Mullemokke*, or "foolish fly" of Crantz (i. p. 86), is the "Molly" of the whalers, the birds which come in greedy crowds to feed on the carcases of the whales. It is the *Procellaria glacialis*, or Fulmar petrel, called *Kakordluk* by the Eskimos, and the black variety *Igarsok*.

[3] The Manx shearwater (*Puffinus Anglorum*) is not an Arctic bird, and is not met with north of the entrance of Davis Strait.

land, the wind decreased to a calm and light N.E. air, and
the ice was very close. On many of the heavy pieces we
saw the bladder-nosed seals (*Cystophora cristata*[1]) lying
basking, and, as we ranged the ship up near them, several
fell victims to our sportsmen. These seals are quite unused
to seeing human beings, for they appeared to take no notice
of the ship beyond raising their heads, and had we been
in pursuit of them, we might have killed any number. I
am surprised that some enterprising fisherman does not
send out a ship or small vessel properly equipped for seal-
hunting. A number of boats sent away from such a vessel
amongst the ice in fine weather might secure a rich harvest
of skins and oil.

In the evening of the 29th, being almost surrounded by
heavy ice, and anxious to get into the land water, I got up
steam for the first time since leaving England. We proceeded
until 9 P.M., when we made fast to a floe to pick up some
seals that were shot in passing, and to get fresh water,
of which we had been sadly in want, owing to our long
passage. We found this water deliciously soft and pure
upon the surface of the floe-piece, and we remained until
11 P.M., when we cast off, and steamed slowly on towards
the land. It was a brilliant night, almost calm, and with
a clear sky, and as we approached the land the ice became
slacker. By 4 A.M., on the 30th, we got into the land water
at about 15 miles distant from the shore. We passed many
seals lying on the ice-floes, and numbers of birds in flocks
were on the ice, in the water, and flying around us.

---

[1] The bladder-nose seal (*Cystophora cristata*) is one of the largest in Greenland. Its name is due to a curious bladder-like appendage on its forehead
connected with the nostrils, which can be blown up at will. The Danish
name is *klapmyd*, the Eskimo *neitersoak* and *nesausolik*.

CHAPTER II.

THE KRYOLITE MINE.

WE were now off the entrance to Arsuk Fiord,[1] the high land of Sermilik bearing N.E. (true), and we could, after a short study of the coast, distinguish Storö, and the two cones of Umanak. The whole coast from S.E. to N.N.E. (true) stood before us like a panorama, and the sea was so calm, and everything so still and peaceful, excepting now and then the rumbling of an overturning berg, or the distant echo of the floes as they pressed together to seaward of us, that it almost seemed like a transition to some other world. It was indeed enchantment, after the constant rolling of the ocean, and the crashing amongst the outside ice, which we had experienced during the previous afternoon. I now determined to proceed to Ivitut[2] to endeavour to get 20 tons of coal, and to steam to Disco in the event of the weather being calm; we therefore turned the 'Pandora's' bow towards Storö, and soon approached the land. We found our late companion, the 'Traveller,' becalmed under the land, and surrounded with loose ice, so I went alongside, and offered to tow her into Ivitut, a distance of 16 miles. Of this offer the Captain gladly availed himself, as he did not otherwise expect to get in for at least two days, there being always a strong surface current running out of the fiords at

[1] This coast is the *West Bygd* of the ancient Norse colonizers of Greenland. Near Arsuk was the old Norse church of Steinnaes. Umanak is the Cape Comfort of our old Elizabethan navigators. Sermilik means "having a glacier."

[2] Or Ivigtot.

this season, caused by the mountain rivers, and the melting of the last remnants of the snow.

When inside the fiord, the wind sprung up and freshened from the S.E., which somewhat delayed us, and we did not arrive off Ivitut until 4 P.M., when, finding that I could be supplied with coal, and not wishing to let go my anchor in 30 fathoms, according to the custom here, I went along-side the barque 'Thor' by the permission of her captain. She was lying alongside a jetty, or rather stage, rigged out from the shore, and was being loaded with kryolite; as she was securely moored, we were enabled to wheel the coal across in barrows. We found Mr. Fritz, the Manager of the Kryolite Company, most obliging and courteous. He offered us every assistance, and any supplies that we might require, besides pressing us to accept his private stock of pigs, which I declined; but he insisted on sending me one small pig for the ship's company, and a large hamper of the most delicious radishes, which he had grown in the open air. Nothing could exceed his kindness, and I wish here to record it, and to mention that anyone going to Ivitut is certain of a hearty welcome and the utmost atten-tion from Mr. Fritz.

We found the 'Fox,' my old ship, lying there, looking quite smart, and evidently kept in good repair. I went on board with Toms to have a look at the old craft which had been our home for two and a-half years, and I felt an in-clination to linger there, and even some desire to exchange for the 'Pandora,' although as yet the 'Pandora' has be-haved in all respects to my satisfaction.

Immediately we were secured I gave leave to all hands, and notwithstanding the myriads of mosquitoes, which ren-dered the shore intolerable, all the men went on excursions, their principal desire being apparently to exchange articles of European manufacture for anything of native workman-

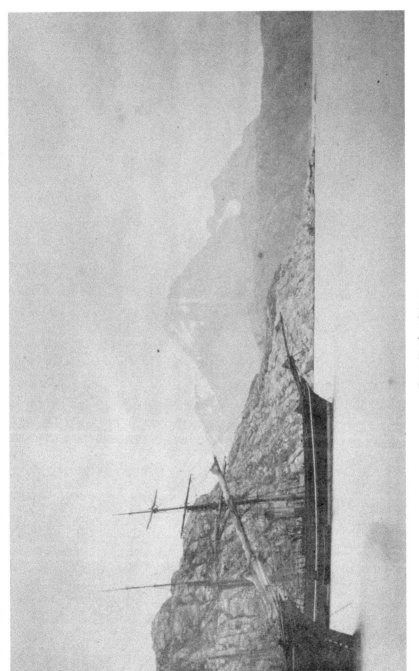

The 'Fox' at Ivitot.

ship, much to the advantage of the natives. They also searched for a cat, as we had left without one, to which circumstance all our head winds were attributed. The result of their search was that we secured at least three cats and a pig. The mullemokke "Billy," which was caught off Farewell, and shorn of its wing, is kept as a pet on board.

Ivitut is situated about 16 miles up the fiord named Arsuk, after the lofty island of that name, which borders the left, or rather the northern side of the fiord, and is composed of granite, with overlying syenite. The granite continues for about 8 miles up the fiord on both sides, when it disappears, and alternates with gneiss. This gneiss forms the shore on both sides of the fiord for from 7 to 8 miles up to the spot named Ivitut by the natives, where the kryolite[1] is found. The name Ivitut (from *Ivik,* grass) was given to this place by the natives on account of its fertility. It was first frequented by them for the purpose of fishing and drying the Arctic salmon, but was deserted on account of the increasing float-ing ice. We owe the discovery of kryolite to a peculiar circumstance. The Greenlanders employed the water-worn fragments of this mineral as weights for their fishing lines, and in this shape the first specimens were sent by the missionaries to Copenhagen as ethnographical curiosities. The kryolite is found near the shore, resting immediately upon the gneiss. The purest is of a snow-white colour, without any intermixture of foreign substances. The grayish-white variety which lies on the surface is considered the second quality of commerce. It very much resembles ice which has been curved and grooved by the action of the sun's rays. The kryolite mines are now regularly worked by a company in Copenhagen, which employs a

[1] Kryolite, or Cryolite, is a very rare mineral found only in the gneiss of West Greenland. It is the double hydrofluate of soda and alumina. The name is from κρυος, hoar frost, and λιθος, stone. It melts like ice in the flame of a candle, hence the name.

manager to superintend the works, and sufficient men are sent out annually to load the ships, which generally obtain a freight—2*l.* per ton—to England or Philadelphia. These workmen are relieved at fixed periods. They do not bring any of their families with them, and generally contract to remain three years, the mines being worked both winter and summer; a smaller mine, more free from snow, being usually worked throughout the autumnal and winter months. The kryolite is used for a variety of purposes, but principally for making soda, and also in the United States for preparing aluminium.[1]

At the time of our visit, the ships 'Thor,' of Hamburg, and the 'Alibi,' of Peterhead, were both loading a cargo, and the 'Traveller,' of the latter place, which we had just towed in, was regularly employed in carrying kryolite to Copenhagen. The 'Fox,' so celebrated in Arctic history, is now in the employ of the company, and is used for bringing out supplies and reliefs of workmen to the colony. The kryolite is all brought from the mine (which is, perhaps, 200 yards from the sea) to the beach, close to the shipping stage, and is stacked in large, square heaps, as being the most convenient for measuring it both for shipment and for the royalty to be paid to the Royal Danish Greenland Company.

I was so occupied on board that I had no time to make more than a very short visit to the mine. I then walked up the rising ground, being attracted by a large wooden cross marking the burying ground of the little colony. It was a well chosen spot, where vegetation flourished, and away from the works and habitations, commanding a lovely view of the fiord and surrounding mountains. The cross

---

[1] For accounts of the kryolite mine, see a paper of Sir Charles Geisecké, in the 'Edinburgh Philosophical Journal,' vi. p. 141; and a paper by J. W. Tayler, Esq., in the 'Quarterly Journal of the Geological Society,' xii. p. 140. These papers have been reprinted in the 'Arctic Manual,' pp. 341 and 344.

bore the beautiful and appropriate inscription taken from Psalm cxxxix., 7–10:

> " Whither shall I go from Thy spirit? or whither
> Shall I fly from Thy presence?
> If I ascend up into heaven, Thou art there: if I
> Make my bed in hell, behold, Thou art there.
> If I take the wings of the morning, and dwell in the uttermost parts
>   of the sea ;
> Even there shalt Thy hand lead me, and Thy right hand shall hold me."

It was with a deep feeling of sadness that I noticed several smaller crosses, marking the last-resting place of the poor colonists who had left their native country to die in this desolate place; and, with an earnest reflection on the above sacred words, I returned on board the ship to obtain a few hours' rest previous to sailing on the following morning.

CHAPTER III.

NAVIGATION ON THE COAST OF GREENLAND.

HAVING received 28 tons of coal, I started at 3 A.M., and steamed slowly out of the fiord. A fog which set in soon afterwards made me very anxious, as the water is too deep to anchor. I had no pilot, and had never been here before, and at one moment I thought of returning to the anchorage at Ivitut, as the only place I could make, but fortunately, on rounding the western extremity of the Island of Arsuk, the fog partially cleared, and we found a fresh S.E. (true) wind blowing out of the fiord, to which we immediately made sail, and passed out to sea without further difficulty. We soon fell in with streams of ice, which were apparently being driven along the coast from the south, and out of the great bays about Julianshaab.[1] The wind also increased, and we ran at some speed under reefed topsails to the northward, avoiding the ice as much as possible, but sometimes receiving a smart blow. Our artist took some hydrographic sketches of the coast, and of the entrance to Arsuk Fiord, which if published will be of some service to future navigators of this fiord, the entrance of which is becoming of some importance, and is most difficult to make from the sea without a knowledge of the appearance of the land. We continued running with a fair wind all the afternoon, though the ice compelled us to deviate greatly from a straight course, and by night it came on thick with rain, and so dark that the floes and floe-

---

[1] The southernmost Danish Greenland colony (in 60° 43′ N.), but not the southernmost settlement. Further south there are the Moravian missions of Lichtenau and Fredriksdal, close to Cape Farewell.

pieces could only be avoided with great difficulty. I was up all night, and hoped for better weather next morning (August 1), but the wind now increased to a fresh gale from the southward (true), and the ice became very close in some of the streams. We continued running through streams along the coast, as to seaward the pack seemed much closer. At 7 A.M. I close-reefed, in the event of our having to round to, but we succeeded in getting into clear water about noon. The barometer had fallen considerably, and I fully expected a heavy gale, especially as the rain began to come down in torrents, and the weather to thicken. In the forenoon we had to haul out of a heavy jam of ice pressed upon a long reef of islands and rocks which extended above our bows, among which the larger pieces had grounded, and had brought up the floe, forming a lee shore of the wildest description. Having cleared the western extremity of this danger, we again bore away, and at noon passed close to the 'Vaidoe Island,' just off the entrance to the colony of Frederickshaab. But the thick weather prevented our seeing more than the outlying isles and rocks, which we passed at one mile distant. In the afternoon we again passed through a very heavy stream of ice, and on approaching the outer edge, I heard the sea breaking violently amongst the floes. I took this as an indication that we were getting clear, and to the northern limit of the Spitzbergen drift ice. Shortly afterwards in getting into more water, we suddenly experienced a heavy swell, and I then knew that we need not expect much more of this troublesome and dangerous enemy. In the evening we were approaching the glacier which extends down to the sea north of the Tallart Bank, and about 28 miles north of Frederickshaab. It is the most conspicuous mark upon the coast of Greenland, and cannot be mistaken. Our artist took a view of it. I remember that when we pushed through the Spitzbergen ice in the

' Fox,' the first landfall we made was this glacier, which immediately directed us to the position of Frederickshaab. In sailing through ice, especially if very close, it is difficult to keep the reckoning, and as such navigation is also often accompanied by thick weather, it is necessary, if possible, to have a sure landmark.

The night proved better than I expected. The wind moderated, but the rain continued in torrents, and we passed through a quantity of drift masses of ice, which I supposed had been hung up by bergs grounded off the Tallart Bank and the glacier. But it was too dark to see anything, and we continued through the gloom with a good look out, the ship rolling with her heavy deck-load, and everything dripping with rain and fog.

(Aug. 2.) The morning broke, thick with rain, but to my great relief no ice was passed. The wind fell off to nearly a calm, and as I fancied we must be near or over the southernmost Torske Bank, I sounded, and found 25 fathoms. We immediately stopped, and put over some fishing-lines, but without success, as a light wind, with a current to the north prevented us from keeping our lines on the bottom. The only things brought up were some conglomerate composed of ascidiæ inside horny cases, and outside the cases bivalve molluscs, and several common log worms.

We steamed to the northward, and during the afternoon I observed many terns,[1] kittiwakies,[2] and a few looms.[3] The surface of the water was frequently rippled as if by a strong current; many pieces of drift ice were also passed, from all which I hoped we were setting to the northward. We passed one large iceberg, apparently aground, about 2 P.M.

---

[1] The Arctic tern (*Sterna Arctica*) is a beautiful little sea swallow with red legs and beak. The Eskimo name is *Imerkoteilak*.

[2] The kittiwake is a graceful Arctic gull (*Rissa tridactyla*, or *Larus tridactylus* of Fabricius). The Eskimo name is Tatterak.

[3] Brunnick's guillemot (*Alca arra*); in Eskimo, *Akpa*.

(August 2); its summit was crowded with birds, which from the distance appeared to be terns, apparently waiting for the fog to clear off to resume their flight. The mist disappearing, we had a lovely night; but the wind continuing light from the N.W. (true) we kept slowly steaming to the N.N.E.

We had been eating some of the seal beef, which we procured in passing through the ice, and it was generally appreciated by the officers, and especially by " Joe," but at present, the crew, as might be expected, rather looked with disdain upon it, and did not seem to care for it. They soon found out its value, as it is certainly the most nutritious and wholesome food in this part of the world, and by steeping it well and boiling it twice over it is, in my opinion, equal to very tender ox beef.

(Aug. 3.) We continued to the northward under steam, the wind still blowing directly against us. At 11 o'clock we saw the islands outside Ny Sukkertoppen,[1] and could make out through the fog the high conical mount which stands out from the mainland, and so well marks the approach to the colony. At noon the wind changed to the south (true). So we ceased steaming, and passed within a mile of the islands off Ny Sukkertoppen, on the largest of which we noticed a white wooden beacon, or staff, with cross pieces at the top. The current ran north, and caused strong ripples on the surface. We now also noticed flights of eider drakes for the first time—they were going seaward, and came in constant flocks from the land.

(Aug. 4.) During the whole of the next day we had a light north wind, with clear sky, mild weather, and a hot sun. I stood in towards the land, coasting about a mile off, until off the entrance to Surk-ström Fiord at noon, when we

[1] " Ny," or New Sukkertoppen (sugar-loaf) is south of the older settlement of Sukkertoppen, which was founded in 1755, in 65° 20' N.

suddenly found ourselves among a labyrinth of reefs and rocks not marked in the chart, which I named Pandora Reefs, and on one of which we touched slightly. I then hauled out to W.N.W. (true), the wind being still northward, and cleared all the dangers. The splendid scenery stood like a panorama before us, and as we passed Surk-ström Fiord our artist made a sketch of this beautiful arm of the sea, which penetrates direct inland 30 or 40 miles, having precipitous mountains on each side 4000 to 5000 feet high, and reaching to the inland ice, which we could plainly see at the head. I then thought of standing off to the Torske Bank to catch some cod-fish, and was proceeding N.N.W., under very easy steam and fore and aft canvas, when on stopping to sound we observed some natives coming off in their kayaks. They had had a long pull, as we were now at least 16 miles from the land; and although we had been standing off at 5 miles an hour, they had never given up the chase, and now overtook us. They brought salmon, fresh and smoked, and a few eggs, and all that the poor fellows asked in exchange for eighteen of these fine fish, was a few biscuits and a little tobacco. They had pulled so hard, that they were quite wet through with the sea, so we hoisted them all in, gave them a good warming in the engine-room, and a glass of grog, and they took their leave quite happy and contented. They belonged to Old Sukkertoppen, but were staying for the present at a place called Kangek,[1] just north of Surk-ström Fiord, catching salmon and reindeer.

(Aug. 5.) I had limited the engineers to 3 cwt. of coal per hour, and we could not therefore steam more than 4 knots. The wind was west (true) alternating with calms until 4 A.M., when a breeze sprung up from the southward, and we set all canvas, and at 8 A.M. stopped the engines. We passed the

---

[1] Kangek means a cape or headland. The name frequently occurs along the coast of Greenland.

Knight Islands off the colony of Holsteinborg,[1] and at noon were in lat. 67° 11′ N. long. 54° 26′ W., steering along the land at a distance of 12 to 14 miles, our artist being busy all day making hydrographic sketches of the coast at the most interesting points. At 6 P.M. we sounded in 18 fathoms, and found shells, sand, and particles of granite.

(Aug. 6.) I was on deck during the whole night of the 5th, as we were passing close to Rifkol, the water being very shallow, and the islands very low. In the morning we had passed Rifkol, and had gone inside the rocks laid down in the chart. The coast here was quite changed in appearance, and the transition from the high snow-capped mountains to a low, irregular tract quite devoid of snow was very remarkable. I had intended on the previous evening to stop at the Rifkol Bank to try to catch some hallibut and cod, and we sounded in 17 fathoms, finding sand, shells, and small stones from the granitic rocks, but a light breeze sprang up, and being so anxious to get onward, I gave up the attempt.

[1] At this time H.M.S. ‘Valorous’ was in Holsteinborg harbour undergoing repairs, after having run upon a reef of rocks not marked on the chart, on July 27. The ‘Valorous’ left Holsteinborg on August 8.

CHAPTER IV.

GODHAVN AND THE WAIGAT.

THE Island of Disco had been in sight since 7 A.M., at a distance of nearly 70 miles. We continued to the N.N.E., passing to windward of the Whalefish Islands and the solitary islet west of the Hunde Islands, upon which we observed thousands of birds, apparently roosting.

The bay of Disco, and the grand cliffs and snow-covered table-land of the island to the northward, were now spread out before us, and to the eastward were Jacobshavn and Christianshaab. Numbers of whales of the finned species were blowing in all directions, and the sea was everywhere dotted with icebergs, the whole forming, in the clear, bright atmosphere, a most enchanting scene. We passed close to windward of the Whalefish Islands, and the two flat islets south of Godhavn, upon one of which we so nearly ran the ' Fox ' in a gale and snow storm in May, 1857. On approaching the high land, the wind fell lighter and more baffling, and, with our slow steaming, it was not till midnight that we arrived off the entrance to Lievely.

(Aug. 7.) On August 7, I observed a whale-boat approaching, and received on board Mr. Elborg, the governor, who had kindly come out to meet us, bringing me letters from Captain Nares and Mr. Clements Markham. I learned that the 'Alert' and 'Discovery' had arrived at Disco on July 6th, after a very severe passage across the Atlantic and in Davis Strait. She had, after staying nine days in harbour, transhipped stores from the ' Valorous,' and proceeded northward on the 15th, intending to stop at Ritenbenk and Upernivik, to ship more

Beach at Godhavn. Eskimo iglu.

Rocks at Godhavn.

The Church at Godhavn.

dogs. The 'Valorous' had left Godhavn at the same time, having proceeded to the coal mine in the Waigat, and intending thence to go southward to make observations in sounding and dredging in Davis Strait. I consequently addressed all letters for that ship to the Secretary of the Admiralty, as there was now no chance of our meeting her. We anchored in Godhavn, but found no other ship there, the Company's vessel having left for home the previous evening; but, as another was expected in about a fortnight, we wrote up our letters, and having filled up some water and given the crew general leave and a dance on shore, we departed at midnight for the Waigat. There I expected to find coal already dug out for us by the natives under the direction of Mr. Krarup Smith, the Inspector of North Greenland, who had kindly undertaken this work for me at the request of Mr. Clements Markham.

(Aug. 8.) On August 8 we were steaming slowly along the south shore of Disco, in charmingly mild weather, which rendered a change of clothing necessary. Thousands of icebergs were around us.

The fisheries of Disco appear to be falling off more and more every year, and recently but few whales have been taken. The seals, moreover, are much scarcer than formerly. I noticed no seal meat or fresh skins, and, in fact, the natives appear to be quite at a standstill, except the few who were away at the large fiord at the west side of the island, catching salmon. Perhaps this apparent idleness may have been the result of their having received a good sum of money during the long stay of the three Government ships.

We steamed leisurely along towards the coaling station, which is on the Disco shore, about 30 miles inside the Waigat. As we opened the straits, a strong north wind blew against us, bringing up so dense a fog that it was with the greatest difficulty we could clear the numerous icebergs.

The season seemed an exceptional one, as from former experience I did not expect to meet with anything like the number of bergs which almost choked up the straits, rendering the navigation very intricate. At midnight we were beset by very thick weather, not being able to see much beyond the jib-boom, and, the water being too deep to hold out any hope of anchoring, we were compelled to proceed, under steam, at a very slow rate until I decided to moor to a promising looking piece, which we went nearly stem on to. It was a berg which had turned over, and was consequently very smooth and slippery. After several attempts it was secured with two large ice-anchors, and I hoped to be able to ride by it until the gale decreased or the fog cleared. We sounded in 58 fathoms, and supposed we were about a mile from the Disco shore (the mountain on the point at the entrance to the Waigat bearing west (*true*), and that the berg was aground; but it afterwards floated with the flood-tide and turned over, and began drifting with us upon a group of other bergs.

(Aug. 9.) I was disturbed at 3 A.M. by the noise of the falling over of the berg, and the officer of the watch rushing down to tell me that it had capsized, taking our anchors a long way under water. I still held on until the rolling of the berg released the anchors, when we were once more compelled to steam off into the fog. During the forenoon the sun appeared and the wind decreased, enabling us to obtain the latitude by means of one of Captain George's artificial horizons on deck. We found that we were a little to the northward of Ujarasusuk[1], the point at which I wished to communicate with the natives, and to present a letter to the Factor with reference to the coaling of the ship. Ujarasusuk is not

[1] From *Ujarak*, a stone. Ujarasusuk consists of two wooden houses and about twenty Eskimo huts. It is about 20 miles from the coal mine of Kudliset, on the Disco side, close to the shore, on an abrupt rocky point. It may be found by the bay between Atanekerdluk and Sakkak, on the Noursoak

marked on the chart.   It lies on the Disco shore, about half-
way between the entrance to the straits and the coal deposits
at Kudliset.   After a little delay we saw two houses, but all
our efforts with the steam-whistle failed to produce any effect
upon the occupants, who were probably taking a good forenoon's sleep, being compelled by the dense fog to remain
inactive.   On a closer approach, however, the good people
of Ujarasusuk were aroused by the whistle; dogs, men, and
women were rushing about, and we were soon boarded by a
kayaker, who informed me that Mr. Jansen, the governor,
would be on shore to receive me.   So I landed, and found
that we were on an outlying station of the Ritenbenk dis-
trict, containing about a hundred people, presided over by
Governor Jansen.   On landing, a letter from Mr. Clements
Markham was handed to me.   It stated that the 'Valorous'[1]
had lately been at the Kudliset mines, and had in five days
taken in 105 tons.   Markham also informed me that the
coals were cleared for us, and the Governor said that I
should meet a sloop which was coming from the mines, and
that I might take from her sixteen men and five women to
assist in loading the 'Pandora.'   At Ujarasusuk there were
a great number of splendid dogs, of which I purchased four,
giving six rixdollars for each, that price including the har-
ness, and some shark's flesh for food.

Proceeding to Kudliset, we met the sloop, took in the
men and women, and arrived at the mines at 7 P.M., anchoring in 7 fathoms, and about a quarter of a mile from the
beach.   We then gave the Eskimos a good supper all round

peninsula, being exactly open.   On Issungoak Point there are two peaks, the
northern very sharp and remarkable, resembling a cairn, and a good mark for
finding Ujarasusuk, as it is 4 miles from Issungoak Point.   Narsak was not
seen in passing, and there appears to be no habitation between Ujarasusuk
and Kudliset.

[1] The 'Valorous' was at anchor off the *Kulbrud*, or coal mine of Kudliset, in
the Waigat, from the 17th to the 21st of July.   In eighty-eight hours the men
got on board 105 tons of coal.

and turned in, the men sleeping in the squaresail on deck, and the females, three of whom were remarkably pretty girls, being stowed away in the chart-room, under the guardianship of an old lady, who was evidently the strictest of chaperones, and would not allow one of them to be out of her sight for a moment.

(Aug. 10.) The next morning was very clear and calm. All hands were sent on shore at 5 A.M., and by dint of real good work we succeeded in getting on board about 40 tons[1] by 7 P.M. We then got ready for sea, intending to start as soon as the crew had taken a few hours' rest, they being much fatigued with the day's work. I found the steam cutter of the greatest assistance in towing the boats to and from our ship. At nine we were aroused by a berg coming athwart hawse, but by veering cable we succeeded in clearing our bows of it. I then settled with the Eskimos who had helped us, and having packed up my letters for England, I sent all the natives away to an empty house about a mile distant.

---

[1] The coal lies imbedded in sandstone underlying the trap formation and close down to the sea-level, in seams of from 1 to 7 feet in thickness. The coal is easily excavated and thrown on the beach, and thence taken to the boats. In the spring, when the ice foot exists, it forms a natural wharf, and a ship or lighter might go almost alongside and take the coal direct on board. An analysis of this coal was made by Professor Fyte, of King's College, Aberdeen, as follows:

Specific Gravity, 1·3848.

Volatile matter	50·6
Coke, consisting of ash	9·84
Carbon..	39·56
	100·00

CHAPTER V.

THE PASSAGE THROUGH MELVILLE BAY.

(Aug. 11.) RISING at four o'clock, I took a last look at the scene. It reminded me forcibly of my former visit in the 'Fox,' which seemed but yesterday, even to the mountain stream which still poured over the summit of the highest ridge, falling in a perpendicular silver line for many hundreds of feet. We were a week later this time, and the season was getting on so fast, that it was with a feeling of relief that I ordered the anchor to be weighed. I felt satisfied with the success of our cruise thus far, and did not anticipate another detention.[1] By the afternoon we had sailed and steamed as far as Hare Island, when the wind suddenly shifted to the northward, and we furled all sails, and continued throughout the night with very easy steam, making slow progress. Arriving the next day (August 12) under Svarte Huk, we made a tack off from within a quarter of a mile of the beach, experiencing a strong northward set as we rounded this extraordinary cape. In the evening we could see Sanderson's Hope, and passed close outside the islands, in fine weather and with light north winds.

[1] On August 11 the latitude was 70° 4' 54" N.; longitude, 52° 59' 30" W.; var. 69° 4'. This places the coast on the Disco Island side of the Waigat farther to the N.E., and altogether different from the Admiralty charts. The coal mine may easily be found if the opposite coast is in sight, even when Disco is enveloped in fog, by observing a very sharp needle peak called Manik, which bears N. 52° E. (*true*) from the mine. Behind the mine two mountains rise to about 3000 feet, with a remarkable stream of water flowing over the highest ridge. The 'Valorous' made the latitude of a position at the coal cliff near where her men were working 70° 3' 24" N.

(Aug. 13.) The morning of the 13th of August was ushered in with light south winds, and I decided to stop off Upernivik to send my last letters home, so we steered in between the two easternmost of the Woman's Islands, and entered Upernivik Bay, rounding to close off the settlement.[1] The Governor came on board, and informed us that the 'Alert' and 'Discovery' had left on the 22nd July, and that he considered it to be a very favourable season for them, although on the day they sailed there was a good deal of ice outside the Woman's Islands and to the northward, which obliged them to steer out west.

Having sent a present of a satin cushion to our old friend Sophia, who is now the wife of the Governor, and purchased a few sealskin clothes and two more dogs, we bore away, the weather threatening from the S.W. and a heavy rain falling, and passed out between the Talbot Reef and the nearest islands, steering away to N.N.W., and continuing through the night under canvas.

(Aug. 14.) At 7 A.M. we could just distinguish the Horse Head, and flocks of looms continually crossed, flying to the westward, from which I inferred that the middle ice was not far out in that direction. We saw numbers of single birds, and hen birds with single young ones, feeding in the water; but the flight of the strong birds was seaward, without resting near the ship. In the afternoon we passed through a

---

[1] In approaching Upernivik two rocks were observed just above water, Sanderson's Hope bearing about E.S.E. (*mag.*) from the westernmost rock, which was about 4 miles to the south of the south Woman's Island. The weather was too thick to allow of any angles being taken. The rocks or reefs are laid down on the plans in the ' Pandora's ' hydrographic book kept for that purpose. In going into Upernivik the two islands off the Hope were left on the starboard hand, and a course was shaped between them and the next one to the northward. In leaving Upernivik the ' Pandora passed to the eastward of the Talbot Reef, which was clearly visible, and then a course was shaped to the N.W. The reef laid down off the south end of the small island on which the colony of Upernivik is situated, is visible by the break of the sea if a good look-out is kept.

long chain of huge icebergs, lying north and south as far as
the eye could reach, and, the weather clearing off, we found
ourselves close to the outermost of the Duck Islands. We
got good observations, placing them in lat. 73° 36′ N., long.
57° 47′ W. There were four islands visible, lying E.N.E and
W.S.W. Snow fell until midnight. We were now deserted
by every living thing.

(Aug. 15.) At 9 A.M. there was a beautiful break in
the sky. The magnificent glacier was also before us, and
Capes Seddon, Lewis, and Walker in sight. A few huge
icebergs were scattered here and there, but we saw no floe-
ice. Being quite out of fresh water, we sent away a boat to
one of the bergs for some loose pieces of ice. The afternoon
was glorious. There was a clear, brilliant sky, and a temperature of 35°. The fog was gone, and only one or two
bergs were to be seen. We had also a constant swell from
the N.W. and W.N.W., and could hardly believe that we
were in the dreaded Melville Bay. It was more like passing
a fine autumnal night on the Atlantic. Near this point, on
August 30, 1857, the ' Fox ' was hampered with the ice, and
finally beset altogether for a winter's drift with the pack.
We reminded ourselves that it would not be wise to " Halloo
until out of the wood." There was, however, no prospect of
meeting the middle pack ice, and we steered a direct course
for Cape York. To my astonishment, the small quantity of ice
we met was completely deserted, and we only saw an occasional
fulmar, no looms, seals, or any living thing ; and the contrast
between the brilliant sun and iceless sea, with the absence
of all life, was most wonderful. We could not have been
far from the middle pack, as whenever the flaws of wind came
from W.S.W. or S.W. the air was raw and cold, and fog with
light snow, or rather frozen particles of mist, came on. Our
latitude at noon was 74° 46′ N., the longitude being 60° 9′
W. We continued slowly through the night, with light

S.W. winds, no ice being in sight except a few bergs. The barometer was 29.65; temperature, 30° to 35° Fahr. We now had occasional calms, and used our steam, going as slowly as possible to save fuel. The ship was so completely covered with long grass as to be rendered almost motionless unless in a fresh breeze, and the low temperature of the water appeared not to have the slightest effect upon it. This was a serious matter, our progress being so retarded that I feared we should not go any great distance in this season. At noon the remarkable peaked mountain to the east of Cape Melville was in sight above the mist which hung to the northward. We were now passing through another chain of grounded icebergs, and I was forcibly reminded of the time when, beset at this season of the year in the 'Fox,' we drifted past this very place, and expected to be driven against icebergs in the same positions as those now before us. Could they be the same? To me it is doubtful, although the same bergs apparently have been seen by former navigators year after year.

At five o'clock our quietude was temporarily broken into by an alarm in the ship. All hands on deck, for Joe had seen a bear swimming across our bows, and had run down for his rifle. A boat was lowered, and Lillingston and myself went away, and returned with a young she-bear about five feet long. Poor thing, she made a gallant swim for it, and it was with difficulty that we overtook her in the boat.

At eight o'clock we arrived near the land in the neighbourhood of Cape York,[1] where we found quantities of smashed-up ice, enormous bergs, and small pieces. It looked as if there had been a heavy gale; but there was too much fog to see any distance towards the shore, which also seemed full of ice. Out to the W. and S.W. the sea was perfectly clear.

[1] Named by Sir John Ross after the Duke of York, on August 16, 1818, His Royal Highness's birthday.

By midnight we had to stop steaming owing to a thick fog, and being beset with small and thin floes apparently of this season's formation. The temperature fell to 28°, and the ice crystals could be seen rapidly forming between the pieces of ice. Our rigging was covered with a white coating of frost. (August 17.) I had hoped that the low temperature in passing through the ice would have killed the weed on the ship's bottom, but was disappointed on the following morning to find it as flourishing as ever.

CHAPTER VI.

THE CARY ISLANDS.

WE were now about 8 miles south of Cape York, and fell in with streams of ice, composed of old floes, and new ice and bergs, extending out from the land towards the S.W. for 10 or 15 miles. After passing the ice, we proceeded towards the Cary Islands, our artist taking sketches of the Beverley cliffs and the Petowak glacier. I forgot to mention that I had sent away a boat the day before, with a small party to shoot *rotches*,[1] of which thousands were feeding among the new ice-floes. The natives come down to Cape York at this season to catch *rotches* in nets for their winter stock.[2] We could not, however, without serious delay, get close in to the land, to see if any natives were there, so I now steered for the Cary Islands, where I expected to find despatches from the 'Alert' and 'Discovery.' We had a fine calm night, with a light southerly air occasionally. We passed Wolstenholme Island, and at 8 A.M. sighted the south-eastern of the Cary Islands in the distance. (August 18.) Towards noon we were drawing near and rising the N.W.

---

[1] The *Alca alle*, or little auk, called *akpalliarsuk* by the Eskimo.

[2] We did not, in passing along the face of the Petowak glacier experience the strong current spoken of by Inglefield, but in the evening we fancied we could detect a slight northerly stream, which I attributed to the flood tide. We had a constant swell, almost as if in the Atlantic. It came from N.W. and S.W. (*true*), and we were even obliged to hook back the cabin doors, which one would imagine a very unusual thing in these seas in fine weather. It must indicate a large expanse of water. The barometer fluctuated but little, between 29.65 and 29.80; temperature about 25° to 30° Fahr.; surface of sea, 34° to 36°.

Isle of the group, making, however, but slow progress, as I limited the engineers to the Waigat coal, much to their discomfiture. The wind springing up from the northward (*true*) and freshening to a strong breeze, we beat up to the north-west island, and lay-to about 2 miles or rather less to W.S.W., having to avoid a sunken rock lying about three-quarters of a mile west (*true*) of the S.W. island, off the north extreme. We also observed a reef above water, with rocks extending a cable length from each end, lying a good mile west (*true*) from the middle of the N.W. island.

I took the first whale-boat, and with some provisions and the two casks of letters for the 'Alert' and 'Discovery,' left the ship and sailed towards a promising bay at the mouth of a considerable river or valley on the west side of the island, and we arrived shortly on the beach, and landed without much difficulty.

I sent the boat round to another little cove about a quarter of a mile to the north-westward for safety. Lieutenant Lillingston, Lieutenant Beynan, and Mr. McGahan accompanied me. We immediately ascended towards a cairn on the summit, and after some tough travelling, and crossing a small glacier, we came to almost level ground, where we found two large cairns. Most anxiously we examined the ground with pick and shovel all round the cairn, but failed to find the slightest trace left by either the 'Alert' or the 'Discovery,' nor were there any signs of the spot having been recently visited. The result of our search merely proved that the large cairn was erected on the 17th of July, 1867, by the men of the steam whaler 'Intrepid,' Captain David Souter, a record stating that " other whale ships " were in sight at the time. Little water to the N.W., " weather excellent, and all well. All the ships are clean.

" The finder will please deposit when found. Deposited in
" the north side of the other cairn is a bottle of rum and
" some tobacco."

(Signed)   " CAPTAIN DAVID SOUTER.

" GEO. A. CRAIG, *Surgeon.*

" CAPTAIN J. B. WALKER, *S.S. 'Alexander.'*

(" VAN WATERSCHOVELT, *Surgeon.*")

Further on in the same paper :

" Visited on the 27th June, 1869, by Captain Walker,
S.S. 'Alexander,' Captain Bruce, S.S. 'Esquimaux.' Find
the liquor in good order, and very palatable. No water to
be seen from the top of the island this day. All clean
excepting the 'Diana,' who secured one fish in the early part
of the season. All well.

" J. B. WALKER.

" CHAS. YULE.

" ROBERT M. G. ANDERSON,
     " *Surgeon S.S. 'Alexander.'*

" Also signed,   GEO. F. DAVIDSON, *S.S. 'Erik.'*

" Captain Jones sitting fatigued in the distance.

" JAMES DEWARS, *Surgeon S.S. 'Esquimaux.'*

" PETER THOMPSON, *Second Mate 'Esquimaux.'*

" The 'Alexander,' 'Esquimaux,' 'Erik,' and 'Camperdown,'
all of Dundee, fast to the ice.

" Au revoir !"

I then examined every elevation of the island, and seeing
a cairn on a small knoll at the extreme N.W., distant about
3 miles, I sent Lieutenant Beynan, with three men, to
examine it; to signal to me if any record was discovered,
and not to open anything themselves. After an absence of

an hour and a half, they returned, having found nothing beyond an old record tin which had been previously opened, and was almost destroyed by rust. On it could be deciphered, in painted white letters, the following :

" RESOLUT . .

and

ASSISTA . . ."

The cairn had also been half pulled down, and a wooden staff which had been erected was broken in two.

Our search merely showed that the islands had been visited by whale ships in 1867 and 1869, and that the N.W. extremity of the N.W island had been visited by the 'Resolute' and 'Assistance' in 1851, when under the command of Captain Austin.[1] I need scarcely express my

---

[1] The Cary (not Carey) Islands were discovered by William Baffin on the 8th of July, 1616, and he named them after one of his patrons, Sir Henry Cary, of the family of Lord Hunsdon. Sir John Ross sighted them on the 20th of August, 1818. The 'Assistance' and 'Resolute,' on their return voyage, after a heavy gale of wind, sighted the Cary Islands on the 21st of August, 1851, and a cairn was observed on one of the most conspicuous heights of the N.W. island. A boat was sent to examine it, in charge of Mr. Clements Markham, then a midshipman in H.M.S. 'Assistance,' and it was found to consist of a pile of stones, with an upright piece of spruce deal 5 feet long and 5 inches broad. The letters I—I M—R D, with the date 1827 were cut on one side, and on the other T M—D K, nearly obliterated. Fourteen whalers were to the northward of the Cary Islands in 1827, and most probably one of them left this cairn. The cairn was built up higher, and a record was deposited in the tin case discovered by the 'Pandora' in August, 1875.

The Cary Islands are in 76° 45' N., and 72° 50' W. Five of them are from a mile and a half to two miles in diameter, three smaller, besides detached rocks. The formation is gneiss, rising to a height of 400 feet above the sea, and there is a rich growth of *Cochlearia Grœnlandica*, and other Arctic plants. The cliffs are breeding places for looms, dovekeys, and rotches, of which the officers of the 'Assistance' shot 900 during August 22. Mr. Markham also found ancient remains of Eskimos, consisting of stone huts, cachés, graves, and a stone fox-trap. (See an account of the Cary Islands at p. 335 of the 'Aurora Borealis,' the Arctic newspaper issued on board H.M.S. 'Assistance' in 1850–51, and published by Colburn and Co. in 1852.)

Great care ought to be taken in approaching the N.W. or largest of the Cary Islands, as several sunken rocks lie to the westward (*true*) of it, and the current of the tide runs strong in the flood to the northward, rendering it

disappointment on not finding any letter or news from the Government Expedition, as Captain Nares had written to me from Godhavn, stating his determination to leave despatches at the N.W. of the Cary Islands, and I had hoped to take home some information as to their progress. I had gone nearly 200 miles out of my way, and consumed 10 tons of coal in my endeavours to reach this point, and to carry out my promise to deliver the letters from England here.

Having carefully examined all round, and failing to find any other cairn, I wrote a letter to Captain Nares, or the Commanding Officer H.M.S. 'Alert' or 'Discovery,' stating that the letters contained in two water tight casks would be found on a knoll above the beach, close to the mouth of the wide river or valley on the west side of the island, and bearing about S.W. from the cairn on the summit. It was now blowing hard from the northward, and was bitterly cold; we had been six hours on the island, so I hastily packed up and descended to the shore, and having carried the casks to the top of the knoll, about 70 to 80 feet above the sea, we deposited them, built a cairn to indicate their position, and tied a comforter to a staff made of one of the boat's stretchers. The casks are well above all chance of the sea ever coming over them, and can easily be found by the directions given in my notice on the summit of the island.

It was now past midnight, and as we could do no more for our fellow-voyagers, we re-embarked for the ship.

(Aug. 19). I rapidly turned over in my mind the nature of our situation. Had I had news from Captain Nares stating that he had gone on positively, I would have decided to

necessary to give any grounded icebergs a wide berth. As far as could be judged by the shore, it was high water on the 18th of August, two days after the full moon, at 11 P.M. A good landing will be found, with northerly to easterly winds, on the west side of the N.W. island, at the mouth of a deep ravine, in which is a river, and a quarter of a mile to the northward of which is a little cove with a beach, upon which a boat can be hauled up.

beat up to Littleton Island, and take the letters on. But in the face of a northern gale, and the season fast passing away, and no information as to where the 'Alert' and 'Discovery' had gone, I considered it far best to leave things as they were and proceed on my own affairs, as, if it were possible by chance that the ships were still southward of us, they would pick up their letters on the way, and if north they would probably send down in the spring for them, if considered of sufficient consequence.

Moreover, had Captain Nares stated decidedly in his letter to me that he would go either to Littleton Island or to Gale Point, I would have pushed on to either one or the other in the hope of finding some news, but he left the question between these two places quite open, and the only certain position named by him appeared to be the Cary Islands. To have gone about from place to place under this uncertainty would have been out of the question, and would have involved my giving up all idea of Lancaster Sound, so I determined to make the best of my way in continuation of our programme, and at 1 A.M. we bore up before a fresh N.N.W. gale, with a high sea which rolled in on both sides of our decks, compelling us to secure the bunker-lids. Not a particle of ice was in sight, excepting a few gigantic bergs aground against the islands, and on the distant horizon. The engines were stopped, and we flew before the breeze to the S.W. at a speed which was quite new to us, and with the first really fair wind since leaving England.

CHAPTER VII.

LANCASTER SOUND AND BARROW STRAIT.

THE fair wind fell off as we sighted the land of North Lincoln and Coburg Island, and we had a moderate N.W. wind through the night, with fine weather. We fell in with ice on the morning of the 20th of August, lying about 30 miles east of Cape Horsburgh and Philpot's Island, and the wind coming from the southward we tacked to the S.E. A thick fog came on shortly afterwards, so we continued to the S.E. until evening, when it lifted, and we saw ice extending out from the land in small and large floes, intermingled with bergs.

(Aug. 20.) Three bears being seen on the ice I went away in the second cutter with Pirie and Beynan, and after shooting the old she-bear and one cub we succeeded in getting a rope round the larger cub and towing him to the ship. Now began a most lively scene. The bear was almost full grown, and it was with some difficulty we got him on board and tied down to ring bolts with his hind legs secured, and notwithstanding this rough treatment he showed most wonderful energy in trying to attack anyone who came within reach, and especially our dogs, who seemed to delight in trying his temper. He was at last secured on the quarter-deck with a chain round his neck and under his fore-arms, and soon began to feed ravenously on—I am sorry to have to write it—his own mother, who was speedily cut up and pieces of her flesh thrown to my new shipmate. I hoped that he was only an adopted child, and the great difference between him

Quarter-deck of ‘Pandora.’—A morning's Bag.

and the other cub warranted this supposition, as, being three times the size of the other, he could not have been of the same litter.

(Aug. 21.) We steered on towards the land about Cape Horsburgh; a considerable quantity of ice lying off this remarkable promontory, or rather point, the glacier running down until almost to the sea level, and projecting out over the low land. There is a singular conical hill to the northward of this glacier, which appears from the sea to be almost isolated. Passing round the floating ice, and grounded pieces, we saw several seals basking in the sun, and, going away with Lillingston and Beynan, I brought on board a large bearded one,[1] which we shot upon a high floe-piece. In towing him off he revived, broke the rope, and disappeared, but shortly afterwards arose, quite dead.

On approaching Cape Warrender,[2] a dense fog came on, and at 10 P.M. I was suddenly called on deck, and found the ship running amongst floes of ice. We immediately backed out, and stood away to the southward (*true*), when the fog lifted for a few minutes, and we saw a close pack extending across the straits as far as was visible from the topmast head. It was a dismal night, dense fog, freezing hard, a cutting wind, and surrounded by floes. I attempted to make fast, but the currents so twisted the floes, that we only increased the risk of being beset; I therefore continued working out to the eastward the whole night, never leaving the deck.

(Aug. 22.) At 4 A.M. the fog cleared off, revealing exactly what I had so much feared; a perfect barrier of ice,

---

[1] The bearded seal (*Phoca barbata*) is the *ursuk* of the Eskimo. It is the largest species next to the walrus.

[2] Cape Warrender, so named by Sir John Ross in 1818, is at the north side of the entrance of Lancaster Sound.

D

extending from Cape Warrender right across the straits; at least, as far as we could see from aloft, and filling Croker Bay[1] right into the land. We had also ice to the eastward, but seeing a lane of water, I stood in to the northward, in hopes of finding a lead inshore in Croker Bay. By 4 P.M. we were completely stopped, and made fast to a heavy floe about 8 or 10 miles off Cape Warrender. This floe was of immense size, extending right into the land, not a drop of water being seen between us and the shore. At seven o'clock we were being surrounded, so I hastily cast off and stood back into the open space through which we had come, and into the middle of the straits. We had Divine Service in the evening; and being completely worn out, and unable to see any way of proceeding, I ordered the ship to be hove-to, and went to take a little rest, the first for thirty-six hours.

Our new shipmate, the bear, made desperate struggles to get over the rail into the sea, but the chain was tightened, and at last he went to sleep.

The 23rd was a bright, warm day. Joe had shot a small seal. We lived on seal and bear (of which we had about 600 lb. hung up in the rigging), preferring it to the salt provisions. Not an opening was to be seen in the ice. We were about in the middle of the straits, and having yesterday made the north shore, now steered over to the south coast, and entering a slack place in the pack, we were enabled after much thumping and some intricate steering, to force our way through the floes and new ice, and reach a clear water off Admiralty Inlet.[2] We made fast to a berg-

---

[1] Croker Bay is on the north shore of Lancaster Sound, west of Cape Warrender. It was so named by Parry in 1819, to compensate for the Croker Mountains which Sir John Ross placed across Lancaster Sound in 1818, and which had to be expunged.

[2] Admiralty Inlet is on the south side of Lancaster Sound, opposite to Croker Bay.

piece, in order to get fresh-water ice, but soon found a very strong current, which towed us back to the E.N.E., towards the pack from which we had emerged, compelling us to cast off before we had completed watering. I was at a loss to account for the barrier across Lancaster Sound, never having heard of a record of any similar pack at this season in this part of the straits. Most of the floes were large and quite fresh, the snow apparently remaining just as it had fallen in the winter. Could the pack have driven out of Admiralty Inlet? or had the straits in this longitude not broken up at all this season? I hoped later to receive reports from the whalers on these points.

Admiralty Inlet was now before us. It is a wide strait, and was apparently open, although from aloft a line of ice was reported on the distant horizon. I was sorely tempted to proceed down the inlet and communicate with the natives, with the object of ascertaining if it led through into Regent's Inlet as I believed, but this report of ice precluded the attempt; and, moreover, we saw a dark sky in the westward off Cape Craufurd,[1] and, therefore, pushed on along the edge of the pack, soon coming to an open sea, with the pack receding to the northward, in the direction of Cape Bullen. The weather began to threaten, and the barometer fell rapidly, and E. to S.E. winds springing up and freshening, we bowled away to the westward, in the direction of Cape Craufurd, with far lighter hearts than yesterday, when our progress seemed to be entirely barred. While at tea we heard a loud crash, and hastening on deck found that we had just grazed an iceberg, which had broken our starboard anchor adrift. Had the ship not answered her helm readily, we must have hit it, and in all probability the 'Pandora's' career would have been ended for ever. The night promised to be gloomy, and I was somewhat anxious:

---

[1] Cape Craufurd is on the western side of the entrance to Admiralty Inlet.

snow fell thickly at 8 P.M., with a gusty S.E. wind. We proceeded with easy steam, ready to put about at any moment. The temperature was only 30°, but the wind was soft and mild. As I anticipated, we passed a most dismal night, the wind increasing and howling in the rigging. Snow and sleet also prevailed as we scudded onward, an iceblink frequently ahead; then the inevitable floe in streams and loose pieces, with the sea dashing over them as we flew between. Now and then the moon shone out, but only to make the scene still more ghastly, for our masts and rigging, decks and bulwarks were covered with ice and snow. At 11 P.M. we caught a glimpse of the land, apparently somewhere between Sargent Point and Cape York.[1] It was only for a moment, and then all was darkness and wind and snow and ice. While we were in this situation our bear gradually worked himself into a state of frantic excitement—getting up to the rail, watching the floe ice rapidly dashing past our side—and in his attempts to get over the bulwarks he released his chain until it was evident that in a few moments he would be free, whether to dive overboard or to run a muck among the watch appeared a question of doubt. The alarm being given by Pirie, who was writing up the deck log, the watch was called to secure the bear, and I fear that during the half hour which elapsed the ship was left, more or less, to take care of herself. The whole watch, besides Pirie with a revolver, and myself with a crowbar, assaulted the unfortunate Bruin, whose frantic struggles and endeavours to attack everyone within reach were quite as much as we could control. He was loose, but by a fortunate event a running noose was passed round his neck, and the poor brute

---

[1] So named by Sir Edward Parry in 1819, after the Duke of York. It is at the western entrance of Prince Regent's Inlet. Parry named another cape, between Admiralty and Navy Board Inlets, on August 31, 1820, after the Right Hon. Charles P. Yorke, grandson of the first Earl of Hardwicke, who was First Lord of the Admiralty from 1810 to 1812.

was hauled down to a ring-bolt until we could secure the chain round his neck and body. I had hitherto no conception of the strength of these animals, and especially of the power of their jaws. Fearing that the iron crowbar might injure his teeth, I jammed a mop handle into his mouth while the others were securing his chain, and he bit it completely through. At last Bruin gave in, and beyond an occasional struggle to get loose, and a constant low growling, he gave us no further trouble. I ought to mention that in the midst of the scrimmage the Doctor was called up to give him a dose of opium, in the hope of subduing him by this means, but having succeeded in getting him to swallow a piece of blubber saturated in chloroform and opium sufficient to kill a dozen men, our Bruin did not appear to have experienced the slightest effect, and the Doctor, who volunteered to remain up, and expressed some anxiety as to the bear's fate, retired below somewhat disappointed.

I was on deck the whole night. The snow turned into sleet in the morning, and we scudded up Barrow Strait, and at eight suddenly saw land. (August 24.) Our compasses were almost useless. We had been threading through the ice. We could not distinguish anything beyond a dark black foot of cliff, about 2 miles away. The ship is about, and stands to the S.E. (true). Gradually the fog and sleet are less dense, and we see by the trend of the coast-line that we are on the north shore, for I cannot say that at first I did not feel sure we were close down upon Leopold Island. On the fog again lifting, we saw about 10 miles of coast about Cape Fellfoot, and at 10 A.M. bore away to the westward again, before a strong easterly wind, passing through streams of heavy ice, which was much broken by the gale of the previous night. We did not feel the full effects of this gale, being sheltered by the pack we passed through. I recollect that in the 'Fox' we were subjected to a much more severe gale when running up the same straits under similar circumstances, with the exception of having 20 or 30 miles of pack ice between us and Baffin's Sea.

The barometer fell to 29.40. We got occasional glimpses of the land until 4 P.M., when all was obscured by a perfect pall of fog. I kept the ship S.W. (true) as we passed what must have been Maxwell Bay, the wind still blowing in gusts from the eastward, and heavy ice coming constantly in our way. Looms were continually flying out to seaward, and occasionally a flock would cross us, evidently making straight into the land, and by these signs and the wind we continued our lonely course, our compasses being useless, and there being no other guide. A dense gloom and fog, with snow, and sleet, prevailed throughout the night, and we could see but a few cables' length, the mist hanging over us like a curtain. I was anxious to get to Beechey Island, to examine the state of the depôt there in case of a mishap, and at 5 A.M. (August 25) we rounded to, after passing through a heavy stream of ice, not being able to determine our position. We had no sun and no soundings, and I could only judge that we were somewhere off the land about Cape Hurd. This was a dark day, with nothing to distract the attention from the damp, cold, and gloom, beyond the occasional trimming of the sails. We were iced-up aloft, and great flakes of frozen snow, and hard pieces of ice frequently came down. I earnestly watched the barometer, and at 6 P.M. the mercury rose one-tenth of an inch, and the wind, which was squally and baffling from the eastward, veered more to the N.E. The looms began to pass us from the north, flying south, and at 1.30 P.M. we caught sight of a patch of snow at the foot of the land, which suddenly appeared as if it had rolled from the heavens, and was not more than half a mile distant. We were off Cape Ricketts, and a magnificent view was displayed before us. The steep, precipitous cliffs appeared to hang over our heads, and all the clefts and ravines and gorges in the neighbourhood were white with drift-snow. Cape Hotham appeared in the distance like a golden mound, the sun being reflected upon its icy summit. No ice could be seen, save a few half-worn bergs, one of which supplied us with enough water for a week's consumption in less than half an hour, its edges being broken off with an axe. White whales and seals swam around, and appeared to gaze at us as if we were some apparition coming out from the gloom, and we seemed to be in another world. Such are the changes in this extraordinary climate. The contrast between the shining sun above, and our sloppy, half-frozen decks and snow-covered rigging was most striking.

CHAPTER VIII.

BEECHEY ISLAND.

WE lighted our stoves below, for the first time since leaving England, giving our damp and cold quarters a good drying up, and raising the temperature below from 38° to 54°, a heat which really felt oppressive. At 8 P.M. we were flying towards Beechey, under steam and fore-and-aft canvas. We attempted to take photographs, and occasionally stopped the ship, but our artist desponded in consequence of the slight movement of the waters, which appeared to us only the merest undulation. He succeeded, however, in getting one or two of the magnificent headlands, as we stopped for the purpose immediately under them. We also tried the lead-line, but could find no bottom at 70 fathoms, close to the shore; there may be from 90 to 100 fathoms, as the lead had been down twice on a hard ground with 120 fathoms out. At 9.30 we sighted Cape Riley and Beechey Island. We saw a cairn with a staff at the south end, and we soon made out a house and boats upon the low shore. The wind increased from the north, with all appearance of a gale. I prepared to anchor, and steered in towards the bay. At eleven we anchored in 12 fathoms, mud and clay bottom, Northumberland House bearing N.N.E. (*mag.*) about a quarter of a mile, and veered to 30 fathoms of cable. It now blew a gale from N. to N.N.W. directly out of the bay. I went on shore with two of the officers to inspect the place, and ascertain the state of the provisions and boats. I found that the house had been stove in at the door and in both sides by the wind and bears, and almost

Cape Riley, where the first relies of Franklin's Expedition were found.

The ' Mary ' at Beechey Island.

everything light and moveable either blown out or dragged out by bears, which had also torn up all the tops of the bales, and scattered the contents around for some distance. The house was nearly full of ice and snow, and frozen so hard that we could not remove anything excepting with pickaxe and crowbar, and even then only the few things which were projecting above the surface. The tea chests were all broken open and most of their contents scattered about. Many of the beef casks had been eaten through the bilges, and the contents extracted. The whole place was a scene of confusion, and the kitchen a mere wreck. I could not find any traces of the place having been visited by human beings since our departure in the 'Fox,' on the 14th of August, 1858. The only thing I noticed was that a coal fire had been made on the beach; but this might have been done by our crew of the 'Fox,' or even by the crews of the squadron of Sir Ed. Belcher. A cask of rum standing in the doorway intact was conclusive proof to my mind that neither Eskimo nor British sailors had entered that way.

I found the 'Mary,' cutter yacht, in good condition; her bottom appeared quite uninjured, but we could not see her garboard for the stones heaped under the bilges to keep her upright. She stood in apparently the same position as when formerly placed there. In her fore compartment is an anchor and chain, some horn lanterns as bright as new, and sundry boatswain's stores. In her main cabin the sails are stowed in the wings, and beyond a slight leakage from the decks the cabin was dry, perfectly clean and free of snow. The after compartment was in a similarly good state, and a set of carpenter's tools and caulking implements were carefully stowed there. The ladder was in excellent order, most of the spars good. Standing rigging was aloft, but no running gear could be found. I should consider that the 'Mary' might be made available for a retreating party in about four or five days with the resources of Northumberland House.[1] The lifeboat cutter lying by her was marked

↑
X X X
W
N—1150
Oct.
1851.

She was in fair condition, and only required the wood ends to be refastened. Her oars and masts were complete, but her sails were partially torn by bears. There were ten copper crutches in her fore and after compartments.

She could be made serviceable in one day. A lifeboat cutter near the house was next examined. She is lying end on to the beach, above high-water mark, and is marked

↑
X X X
W
N—1151
Octo
1851.

She also was in good condition, and only required refastening and caulking. There were ten brass crutches in the compartments, and the oars and masts were in and outside the house. The sails were not seen, but were supposed to

[1] Northumberland House on Beechey Island, named after the then First Lord of the Admiralty, was built by Commander (now Rear-Admiral) Pullen when in command of the 'North Star,' which ship wintered there in 1852-53 and 1853-54, as a depôt for Sir Edward Belcher's expedition. The house was built in the autumn of 1852, of lower masts and spars taken from the American whaler 'M'Lellan,' which was crushed by the ice in Melville Bay in 1852. Sir Leopold M'Clintock visited the house and examined the stores on August 11, 1858.

The Graves of Franklin's Expedition.   Beechey Island.

Franklin and Bellot Monument and Post Office.   Beechey Island.

Northumberland House.   Beechey Island.

have been torn up by the bears. This boat could also be made serviceable in one day, and is in an easy position for launching.

A whaleboat on the south side of the house unserviceable. The iceboat on runners could be easily made serviceable. The flagstaff is standing all right, and the arrangement for pointing the direction (*true*), in good order, but there is no vane or arrow.

I found the pedestal in good condition, and also the marble tablet in memory of the Franklin expedition, the brass plate which M'Clintock fastened on it being quite bright, as if the bears had been lying on it.[1] The record box was hanging to a beam in the house, and having examined the original list of provisions, and M'Clintock's record, which was as fresh as if just written, I took a copy of it, and removed all the documents to the post office in the pedestal, for safer keeping, and in which I found only a memorandum from Sir E. Belcher.

(Aug. 26.) At 8 A.M., the wind having partially moderated, we commenced to clear some of the ice and snow; and having with great difficulty found such provisions as we were actually in need of, and thirteen bags of coal, of which there still remained at least 10 tons, I placed a record of our proceedings in the pedestal, with a list of the provisions taken away, and embarked at 7 P.M., having carefully repaired and closed the house. Our artist was busily employed all day in taking photographs of every object of interest, and Mr. Beynan was sent to the summit of the island to report on the ice. He could not see any from any visible point in the horizon, but in the south-west a mist was hanging which prevented the completion of his observations.

---

[1] See M'Clintock's 'Fate of Franklin,' p. 173.

CHAPTER IX.

PEEL STRAIT.

HAVING got all the boats up, we weighed anchor at 8 P.M., and stood away to the southward for Peel Strait, the wind being fresh from the N.W. (August 27.) At 4 A.M. we were among loose ice, and at noon a heavy pack stopped our progress, when I made fast to a floe to await the clearing of the fog, which soon lifted, enabling us to proceed under steam through the pack, which extended as far as we could see along the north shore of North Somerset, and particularly off Cape Rennell and about half-way across Barrow Strait, lying in an easterly and westerly direction. As we pushed on, the ice became more open, and by 5 P.M. we were steering through navigable lanes towards Limestone Island, which we could just see from aloft, topping above the icy horizon. We were off Cunningham Inlet, and Cape Hotham,[1] with Griffith Island[2] in sight, to the northward. We ranged up to an enormous "ursuk" (bearded seal), nearly as large as a walrus, for which we at first took him; but he was lying on a very small piece of ice, and although our bullets went through him, he floundered into the sea, and did not rise again. We thus lost at least 500 lb. of good meat and oil.

Our bear was getting more reconciled to his confinement; but when we were among close ice, he got into a state of fury in his endeavour to get out of the ship, and our dogs were constantly worrying him by stealing his food.

---

[1] Cunningham Inlet is on the coast of North Somerset. Cape Hotham is the S.E. point of Cornwallis Island, forming the western side of the entrance to Wellington Channel.

[2] The expedition of Captain Austin, consisting of the 'Resolute,' 'Assistance,' 'Pioneer,' and 'Intrepid,' wintered off Griffith Island in 1850–51.

At night we came to a solid barrier of ice, extending out from the land about Cape Rennell to the W.N.W. (true), as far as could be seen from aloft, with a bright icy sky from south round to N.W (*true*). We then made fast to await a change.[1] I determined to wait at least twenty-four hours, and if we could not then pass, to bear up for Regent's Inlet and Bellot Strait; but at 8 A.M. (August 28) the ice slackened a little, and by 10 we pushed through a small lane which ultimately led us to Limestone Island.[2]

Our artist took more photographs and sketches while we were fast to the floe, and we took the same opportunity to fill up with fresh water, and give the dogs a run.

This morning it was freezing hard, with a temperature of 27°, and our rigging was completely covered with rime; but dark clouds now arose in the south-west, the barometer began to fall, and the wind to arise from the eastward to E.S.E. Finding a land water round Limestone Island, I hauled into the N.E. entrance, and landed to examine the stores which were said to be at Cape Bunny. It was raining heavily, with gusts from the mainland, and occasional sleet. I landed, and hauled up our boat on a shelving beach composed entirely of loose limestone pebbles, and at once proceeded to the low point (Cape Bunny), but could not find anything. Having sent the Doctor and Beynan round the beach, I ascended the gradual slope or ridge leading to the summit of the island, and when about three-quarters of a mile from the point, and at an elevation of about 300 feet, I descried a cairn, evidently built by civilized hands, the

---

[1] We sounded in 110 fathoms while fast to the floe, bottom limestone mud, about 7 miles off the land, Cunningham Inlet, E.S.E. (*true*). Before the change in the weather, the red sandstone hills about Cape Anne (on the mainland of North Somerset, opposite Limestone Island) presented a brilliant reddish glow from the reflection of the sun, and reminded me of the Highlands when the heather is in full bloom on a bright day. On the other hand, the transition to the limestone was clearly defined, the latter presenting the usual dull and gloomy appearance so well known to Arctic travellers.

[2] Limestone Island is on the east side of the entrance to Peel Strait.

ground having been excavated to form the base, and the top being composed of loose stones. Much to my disappointment, we dug up this cairn without finding anything, and I cannot conjecture by whom it was built, or for what purpose. I then mounted to the top of the island on the south face, an elevation of 600 feet by aneroid, but the squalls of wind and rain prevented my getting a good view of the sea. I noticed, however, that the main pack had already moved off from the land to a distance of about 3 miles, but that it still extended round in a southerly or S.S.W direction until shut in by the land against Cape Pressure. As I descended, the rain came down in torrents, and we found it cold work rebuilding the cairn, to which we added some large stones, to make it conspicuous, and having searched the ground all round, and especially on the magnetic north side, without success, I deposited a record in a tin box. I cannot think why we could not find the provisions. I had always supposed that there is but one Cape Bunny, and that it was here that the stores were landed, but there were certainly none to be found on the island.[1]

The Doctor having reported finding remains of ancient Eskimos, I proceeded towards the beach on the south of

[1] In the spring of 1854, when it was unknown whether parties from the 'Enterprise,' under Captain Collinson, might not make their way up Peel Strait from the' westward, Sir Edward Belcher ordered two officers, with sledges, to go to Cape Bunny, on Limestone Island, and deposit a depôt there, in case any parties from the 'Enterprise' should come that way.

Mr. Herbert, a mate of H.M.S. 'Assistance,' left the 'North Star' at Beechey Island, crossed Barrow Strait on the ice, and reached Limestone Island on April 1, 1854. He buried a depôt, consisting of 370 rations of bread, pemmican, bacon, and rum, and 473 of all other stores, on a spit of the eastern extreme of the island, covering it high up with shingle. He also left a flag and staff with a cylinder attached, containing a notice. Mr. Herbert returned to the 'North Star' on April 9.

On April 3, Mr. Shellabeer, the second master of the 'North Star,' arrived at Limestone Island with a second depôt, consisting of 396 rations of small stores, 436 of rum, and 296 of biscuit and meats. He deposited these stores with Mr. Herbert's depôt at Cape Bunny, built a cairn on the high part of the spit of the island, and left a bamboo on it, also depositing a notice. He left a list of the stores in a cairn over the depôt. Mr. Shellabeer returned to the 'North Star' on April 11.

the island, and saw immediately under the precipitous cliffs
which shelter the spot from the north winds, about ten
circular rings of unusually heavy stones, which had formed
the foundation of summer tents, also several cachés made of
heavy stones, oblong, and floored with flat cakes of limestone.
Quantities of bones of the seal, walrus, and whale were lying
about, but we saw no other relics except what appeared to be
a piece of charred coal, which I took on board.

During our absence, the man left in charge of the boat
saw a seal crawl up on the shore, close to him; but, notwithstanding that he had a revolver and ammunition, it is almost
needless to say that he did not get it. We noticed the tide
ebbing from the time we landed at 3.30, until we re-embarked
at 5.30, when it was apparently nearly low water by the
shore, the current having continued running about three
knots to the northward through the channel between the
island and the main.

I embarked with an anxious mind, for the wind was increasing to a gale, the weather thickening fast; we were
drenched with rain and very cold, and the prospect from the
top of the island was not very encouraging. However, I was
determined to persevere, and to push into Peel Strait if possible. I ordered the ship to be steered through the channel
between the island and the main, and having changed my
clothes in our snug and warm cabin, I went on the damp,
dreary deck again. We passed through the channel, sounding in 30 fathoms, about a quarter of a mile off the extreme
point of Cape Bunny, and finding a strong current running
through from the southward. The night was one of the
most dreary I ever passed at sea, and I have had my share.
The wind continued in fitful gusts, rain and sleet in torrents,
thick mist, no soundings, no compass, land on one side and
ice on the other. We could just distinguish the foot of the
land and cliffs, as we passed close under them, by the dark
line over the gleam of the grounded ice. By nine it was

dark. We furled all sails, and steamed against the gale, edging off to the ice as a more secure guide for our course than the land, which we could not follow. By eleven it was so thick that we could literally see nothing but the occasional sheen of the ice as we passed along it on the starboard hand. Anxiously (August 29) I waited for light; but it was three o'clock before we could fairly see, and about four a lift in the mist enabled us to see that we were off Cape Granite,[1] and steering a fair course along the land. By seven we were off a wide bay, the land receding from about 10 miles south of Cape Granite, with a fringe of islands north and south, and forming the line of coast. Our patent log was put over, and on the mist clearing in the westward we saw the land to the W.N.W., about Lyons Point and Cape Biggs.[2] The wind had now come round to W.S.W. and west, but as yet we saw no sun to guide us, or by which to take any angles or directions; so we continued along the coast-line, the ice receding, and there being none visible in the W.S.W. or south. The barometer rose to 29.95 with an appearance of better weather, and we seemed to have arrived in another climate, and also in an iceless sea, for the cold sting was gone from the air, and only a few small pieces could be seen. The land was quite exposed and devoid of snow, excepting occasionally in the interior, in which direction we sometimes got a glimpse of snow patches.

We did not see the small island marked on the chart in the middle of the strait. By 2 P.M. we had passed Howe Harbour, and were off a projecting point not named by Sir James Ross, which is merely noticed as having a lake upon it. Passing within half a mile, we tried for soundings, but could find no bottom with 120 fathoms. I supposed this to be

[1] Cape Granite, on the eastern shore of Peel Strait.

[2] Lyons Point, on Prince of Wales Island, is on the west side of the entrance to Peel Strait. Cape Biggs is on the same side, a few miles farther south.

Hummock Point, and noticed a rookery of skuas[1] on the face of the granite cliffs—they were sitting on the rocks in hundreds. The vegetation formed an extensive green patch, extending from near the summit to high-water mark, or where the ice forms. We kept a good look-out on the shore by means of a powerful astronomical telescope, and cairns were frequently reported to me; but on inspection they proved to be granite boulder stones, with which the coast, and especially the ridges, are strewn.

At 10 P.M. I returned on board from visiting the cairn built by Sir James Ross and Sir L. M'Clintock on Cape Coulman. We found it without difficulty, as we passed close along the coast from point to point. Landing on a small piece of ice, we ascended to about 150 feet, and found the copper cylinder containing the following record:

"The cylinder which contains this paper was left here by a party detached from Her Majesty's ships 'Enterprise' and 'Investigator,' under the command of Captain Sir James C. Ross, Royal Navy, in search of the expedition of Sir John Franklin, and to inform any of his party that may find it that those ships, having wintered at Port Leopold, in Long. 90 W., Lat. 73° 52′ N., have formed there a depôt of provisions for the use of Sir John Franklin's party sufficient for six months; also two very small depôts about 15 miles south of Cape Clarence and 12 miles south of Cape Seppings. The party are now about to return to the ships, which, as early as possible in the spring, will push forward to Melville Island, and search the north coast of Barrow Strait, and, failing to meet the party they are seeking, will touch at Port Leopold on their way back, and then return to England before the winter shall set in. "JAMES C. ROSS, *Captain*.

"7th June, 1849."

[1] The most common skua in the Arctic regions is the *Catharacta parasitica* (or *Stercorarius parasiticus*), mentioned by Fabricius, and by Crantz, i. p. 86; the *Isingak* of the Eskimos.

This simple paper, given as the record of a mere visit to the spot, really shows what a remarkable journey Ross and M'Clintock made when they travelled on foot from Port Leopold round this unknown coast, in the days when sledge travelling was in its infancy.

It contains no claims to the discovery of Peel Strait, nor any mention as to the state of the ice or land to the southward; and although a doubt appears to have existed in the minds of the travellers as to whether it was really a strait or not, yet they seem to have preferred to leave the question doubtful rather than mislead any future voyager.

It also shows how strange are the chances of Arctic navigation, for Ross was in the exact track of the 'Erebus' and 'Terror,' and but one season in rear of Franklin's party having abandoned their ships, and yet Ross's impression must have been strongly against the probability of Franklin having passed down the strait, otherwise he would have expressed his intention to follow this route with his ships in the ensuing summer, rather than the north shore of Barrow Strait.

It was in 1859, in the month of June, that, having completed the journey round the south-west coast of Prince of Wales Land, I again started from the 'Fox' and reached Browne's [1] farthest on the north-west side of these straits, and thence, in crossing over to this eastern shore, I met with so much water on the ice that I was prevented from reaching Ross's Cairn, passing about four miles southward of it. I returned to the ship with the greatest difficulty, having found the ice between this point (Cape Coulman) and Bellot Strait flooded with water to such an extent that we were travelling knee deep in it, and almost floating the sledge itself. I thus missed seeing the cairn, but I can claim to

---

[1] Lieutenant Browne was the second Lieutenant of the 'Resolute,' under Captain Austin. He led an extended sledge party from Cape Walker down the western side of Peel Strait in the spring of 1851.

have discovered, under M'Clintock's command, the land on both sides of these straits southward of Browne's farthest on the western shore, and southward of the point or cape about eight miles south of this cairn on this or western side, and to which point Ross walked, having left his party to build the cairn on Cape Coulman during his absence.

We saw a number of white whales in the bay immediately south of Cape Coulman, and also picked up several horns of the reindeer here. Having left a copy of Ross's record, with another of our own, I took away the original paper, and after carefully closing the cylinder, deposited it in its former place, and we returned to our ship, and steamed towards the next cape, distant about 8 or 9 miles to the southward, and the wind being southerly and the flood tide against us, we went slowly, with all sails furled.

We passed Four River Point about 10 P.M., and, a thick fog coming on, had to lay-to for the remainder of the night. At 5 A.M. we passed outside the islands lying off the coast, and found a wide stream of ice extending east and west across the strait, passing through which we came again into a large expanse of water. But an icy sky southward, and a chilly feeling in the air, warned us that we were approaching a large body of ice, and by 4 P.M. we came to the pack edge, about a mile to the northward of Levesque Island, and extending from the shore 4 miles north of False Inlet, or Fitzroy Inlet, in a concave form, round to the western shore. From the masthead we could see nothing to the southward but a solid pack, and a bright icy sky beyond, and a solitary iceberg about 10 miles south of us, for which I could not account as it is foreign to these straits, and must either have been driven down Barrow Strait or M'Clintock Channel from the north-west. This berg was important, as bearing upon the movement of the ice here.

CHAPTER X.

AN IMPASSABLE BARRIER.

IT was with a heavy heart that I made fast to the floe, about a mile and a half from shore. We were in lat. 72° 14', and close to my former encampment when travelling in June, 1859, from the 'Fox,' then in Port Kennedy. Islands, coast, and ice appeared familiar to me, and I could recognize all the points of interest which we observed during that dreadful march, when, wading up to our thighs in water, and nearly broken down with the fatigues of three months' continuous travel, I barely reached the western entrance of Bellot Straits. I can now account for our having then passed Ross's Cairn without seeing it, as it was we found it with difficulty, even with all hands in the ship on the look-out and at our leisure, for it is not built upon the upper ridge of the point, and is quite concealed from view from the south, and upon almost every bearing. On the former occasion we were pressing on for our lives, and having passed Cape Coulman without distinguishing the cairn in the misty weather, it was utterly impossible to return even a yard.

By seven o'clock, the 'Pandora' entered upon my own surveys, and, with some interest, combined with anxiety, my own chart was brought out for our guidance, and for corroboration, and I was surprised, considering the extremely difficult circumstances under which I was travelling at the time it was drawn, to find how correctly the islands, and also the main land, which was sketched under still greater difficulty by Sir James Ross, were laid down. We made such corrections as were found necessary, and these have enabled us to give a tolerably correct plan of the strait as far as we went.

We were not destined to enjoy much repose, for at 8 P.M. the loose ice through which we had passed in the forenoon began to settle down on us, and we were compelled to cast off from the beach, and steam again to the northward into clear water to escape from being beset. We saw Cape Bird,[1] distant about 15 miles, and the ice appeared to be jammed into the shore as close or even tighter than off Fitzroy Inlet, where we were. We sounded in 93 fathoms, finding a sand bottom.

(Aug. 31.) We lay-to the whole night, off the pack edge; a dense fog set in at midnight, lasting until 5 A.M., when we discovered that we had drifted close to De la Roquette Islands, and I landed upon the largest of the four to deposit a record and view the ice, getting with difficulty through the young and loose ice which was forming between the floes.

From the summit of the island, 200 feet high, we could see one unbroken pack extending from shore to shore, and as far as the visible horizon to the southward, and so close that no ship could penetrate beyond a few lengths into it. The ice had also drifted, during the last twenty-four hours, up both shores to northward, and we were in a deep bight, to get out of which we should have to retire as far as Barth Island. We could plainly see the entrance to Bellot Strait, and the ice was tight packed on the shore there, holding out no hopes of our being able to get out in that direction, or I should have been glad to have held on there upon the chance of some change taking place. Our prospect is gloomy in the extreme—we cannot go south, and I am loth to turn back, yet there is nothing else to be done, for a boat could not get through the pack, and to attempt to travel over it would be fatal. We built a conspicuous cairn on the summit of the

[1] Cape Bird, the farthest point seen by Sir James Ross from Cape Coulman, is on the north side of the western entrance to Bellot Strait.

largest island, and placed in it a record of this our, I fear, most southern position, and, with a sad spirit, I descended to the boat. We observed the dip to be 88° 30′.

We lay-to all night, a mile or two from Roquette Islands, and in the bight of the pack, which now extended northward along the shore of North Somerset nearly to Barth Island, and westward to about the same latitude, the surface of the sea freezing all (September 1) night, and presenting in the morning a glazed appearance all round. A fog commenced about 1 A.M., and at two was quite dense until eight, when I stood back to Roquette Islands. The wind remained southerly throughout the day, with intermittent fogs, and I made several preparations to land on the island to obtain another view of the ice, but it was not until 6 P.M. that we could get through the loose ice surrounding it. A strong south wind was blowing on the other side of the island, and the ice was rapidly sailing up past the group, I had therefore only time to run up to the top and get a hasty glance to the south before I found it imperative to make all haste to the boat and push off to the ship, which was already surrounded by floes, and we were nearly cut off from her. We at once commenced to free ourselves from the pack, and steamed northward for about 3 miles, when we again lay-to.

I observed no change from the island, excepting that the immense pack southward was moving towards us, and the berg which the night before last was about 10 miles away to the southward was now nearly up to the islands. I could see no water beyond a few cracks in the first 5 miles, and the ice had gradually crept up the shore, reaching nearly to Barth Island; and to the westward, still farther north. We were still in a deep bay in the ice. All southward one unbroken pack across from side to side. Fitzroy Island full. Bellot Strait packed close in; and there is no hope of getting farther south. I was most anxious about our position, and if possible to reach Bellot Strait, because there we could run through and await the ice movement northward, and perhaps proceed southward after it had passed, but from here we must have inevitably gone northward if the pack continued to advance in that direction. To winter here would have been useless, as we could not possibly have done more than M'Clintock and Hobson did by travelling over King William Island with the spring and winter snow on the ground; and, moreover, we must have abandoned the ship in the spring before the water made on the floe, as we could not depend upon getting the ship out next summer. I was very loth to turn back, and struggled on, almost against hope, either to reach Bellot Strait or to proceed southward. We had not many hours to make up our minds, but I was inclined to give it another day's trial; and then, if we perceived no favourable movement in the ice, to retreat by Peel Strait, in which case even, we should have to get through the pack which almost closed the northern entrance. To remain here at this season was out of the question. We were hourly in danger of being beset in the pack, and if we could not reach Bellot Strait on the following day, I decided to consider seriously our retreat to the northward.

Thus all my hopes were dashed to the ground; we were helpless, and could not proceed by any human possibility—no boat could get half a mile through this ice, nor could one walk many yards in it. It was a dense mass of small divided floes, intermingled here and there with large old floes. To travel on the land was equally impossible, and especially without the ship being fixed in some known and secure position, and a boat would be required even then in order to cross from Boothia to King William Island.

I now almost gave up all hope of our making the North-West Passage this year; and, indeed, was more than ever of the opinion that the only way to accomplish it would be to proceed by way of Bellot Strait, there awaiting the moving of the pack northward, and then pushing as fast as possible down to Cape Victoria, for I thought that if the northern part of Peel Strait was *entirely* free of ice, as we had found it, the pack would be to the southward, as it was impossible that 120 miles of ice could have dispersed, and it was more probable that it swayed backwards and forwards, northward and southward in the straits, until arrested by the frosts of September. We were evidently on the northern edge of it, and as it probably impinged about the Tasmania group,[1] we could not hope for a passage unless with a south (*true*) or S.S.E. wind; and then we should be, in our present position, carried back with it. Once only in Bellot Strait, where we could hold on, I believed that this southerly gale, which was evidently blowing with great force beyond our visible horizon, would eventually move the ice up northward until we could go on; but I could see no hope of reaching Bellot Strait, for although its entrance could be plainly seen, I could detect nothing but one mass of ice closely packed along the shore.

Neither could I see any hope in the western horizon, for when we attempted to go in that direction we were headed off until we found ourselves steering north, and without any indication of any lead of water along the shore of Prince of Wales Land.

We got several seals, and also shot a quantity of mullemokkes for the dogs.

Numbers of white whales were constantly around the ship, but although we twice lowered a whale boat, with harpoon, gun, and line, we did not succeed in securing one. On visiting Roquette Island to-day, we discovered a remarkable

[1] The Tasmania group, on the west coast of Boothia, is at the south entrance of Franklin Channel, which is the southern continuation of Peel Strait.

My last look at the North-West Passage, Sept. 2nd.

pool or small lake near the summit, completely surrounded by mosses, and forming an entire circle. We also saw quantities of the dung of reindeer and several looms, thus proving that the deer must cross to these islands on the ice in search of food.

Seeing that the ship was being fast enclosed in the drifting ice, I hastened down to the boat, and only arrived on board in time to get the ' Pandora ' clear of the island, as the ice-floes were swimming round her; and we had to back in close to the beach before we could get her head the right way. A gale now commenced from the southward, with sleet, snow, and mist, and the northern edge of the pack began to break away and fly before the wind. There was only one course to pursue to prevent being beset, viz. to run before the gale and outstrip the sailing floes, which had already preceded us on either hand.

CHAPTER XI.

A PERILOUS RACE WITH THE ICE.

(Sept. 2.) WE passed a dismal night, drifting with low sail to the northward before the gale, in company with large and small floes and fields of ice, which gleamed through the darkness, and gave a weird appearance to the sea. We could not perceive anything at a distance of more than half a mile, and had constant alarms of a pack ahead, which, however, proved to be only streams of ice. By eight in the morning we had for half an hour a clear view, and I could see that we were close up to Barth Island, Roquette Islands being in the horizon, and surrounded by pack ice. By noon the wind came round to north, and blew a fresh gale with snow, and a new phase came over the scene, for quantities of ice of a different description were coming from the northward, viz. fresh, unbroken fields of a year's growth, and with the smooth snow on the surface. I could not imagine where all this fresh ice came from, unless out of Browne's Bay;[1] it appeared to fill the straits northward of us, and we worked to windward the whole day, until up to Olrick Island, when we still saw more and more ice coming down, apparently filling the straits, leaving only a small space between the island and the shores of North Somerset; and having reached this water, we commenced to dodge about for the night. I close-reefed the topsails, as they froze so fast after any rain or sleet, that we should have been in great trouble if we had had to shorten sail suddenly, and I therefore meant to keep in the reefs until we were short of coals.

[1] A deep bay on the west side of Peel Strait.

The barometer had oscillated in a curious way during the last thirty-six hours, having fallen to 29.60, and rising at 8 P.M. to 29.85, with a dark gloomy sky, and a strong N.N.W. wind. On the 3rd of September we stood back towards the western land, having cleared the northern edge of the loose ice; but we soon met again a quantity of ice under the western shore, which quite frustrated my intention of landing and obtaining a view from the high cliffs. The wind came on at the same time from the southward, and began to blow in squalls, with snow and sleet. From the topmast head I could see nothing but a dense pack of ice southward of us, and all that we had been passing was arrested by the block of what I still thought was pack ice across the strait from Kennedy Bay to the southern point of Bellot Strait. There seemed no hope in that direction, and I reluctantly bore away to the northward before the gale.

This was a sad blow to all our hopes. On the previous Sunday we were running through these straits, with a clear sea, and with not a sign of ice; on Monday we passed Barth Island whilst at dinner, and by four o'clock were arrested at the Roquette Islands by an impenetrable pack. Shortly afterwards I obtained a view from the summit of the largest of this group and could not see a drop of water to the southward, it being one sheet of ice across from side to side, and as far as the visible horizon—16 miles—for we were at an elevation of about 200 to 250 feet. As we had the spring tides of the new moon I hoped that it might give way, but after lying four days about the edge of the barrier, no change had taken place, and I had already given up all hope of passing south this season, for I felt convinced that the pack ice extended right across from Kennedy Bay, towards the Tasmania group.

We had gone within 140 miles of Point Victory, and it was too provoking that we could not even proceed that distance, if only to return this way; but I saw no hope, and therefore sailed northwards again.

On the 3rd we had the temperature about 27° to 28°, with barometer 29.60. We passed Howe Harbour about 2 P.M. and continued northward under reefed sail until 8 P.M., when being close to the land southward of Wadworth Island, we tacked to the northward, and sounded in 80 fathoms, mud and sand bottom.

(Sept. 4.) I revolved in my mind the best course to pursue. To return southward again seemed hopeless, as we should only arrive at the edge of the pack which lay to the north of the fast ice in the straits, and which when we left it had accumulated up to Barth Island. We had already lost 10 miles of ground, as it was impossible to remain in the position we first reached at the Roquette Islands from having no harbour or bay in which we could anchor, and from the ice constantly coming down upon us from the north and compelling us to fleet up clear of it, which I did, in order to prevent being beset in a position in which we must necessarily have abandoned the ship the next spring, and have travelled to Fury Beach, Port Leopold, and possibly Beechey Island, and therefore we could not even attempt to explore King William Island by sledge parties, which, even if possible, could not have resulted in finding any remains of the Franklin Expedition beyond those obtained by M'Clintock and Hobson, who had made an exhaustive search, and whose footsteps we could only follow. To remain in the strait for the winter would certainly have involved the loss of the ship, as we could not afford to wait until the following August upon the chance of coming out, as the northern part of Peel Strait was evidently only occasionally open. To proceed round by Regent Inlet to Bellot Strait appeared an alternative, but we had already seen at least 10 miles of solid ice southward of Bellot Strait, right across Franklin Channel, with a bright ice sky, and no probability of getting southward this year by that route, in time to pass through to Behring's Strait. I was reluctantly beating to the northward all the forenoon against a northerly wind and in a close sea, and by noon we were again off Cape Granite, finding a wonderful change in the appearance of the land. When we passed down the strait a week before we could see scarcely a vestige of snow, except upon the higher lands in the interior, but now even down to high-water mark, the land was so white as to appear like ice through the mist.

By 5 P.M. we began to see ice in the north-west, and so furling square sails, and steaming easily with fore-and-aft canvas, with the wind N.W. to W.N.W., we gradually drew up to Limestone Island, but a change now occurred; the wind began to blow in heavy gusts, with dense showers of snow, between which we could just catch a view of a solid pack to the westward, and of Limestone Island to the N.E. We passed close round Limestone Island, the cliffs towering over us through the snow, and the pack being scarcely half a mile to westward. The barometer fell rapidly to 29.50, and at the same time the temperature fell to 24° as we brought the pack to windward of us. I could just distinguish at intervals what appeared to be a sort of land water, about a mile wide, and I determined to run a race with the pack, and try to pass Cape Rennell before it impinged completely on the land. This was our only chance of getting out of the strait, for had we hesitated, or stood back to the south-west, we should certainly have been shut in for the winter. We therefore pressed on into the gloom of the fast increasing darkness, and experienced a dreadful night, the wind increasing to a gale from the N.W. with dense sleet, hail, and snow showers in blinding drifts. To stop was impossible, for the pack, which was to windward, and seemed to be composed of enormous floes, unbroken for miles, was evidently coming in on the land, whilst on the other hand we constantly found streams of ice already jammed in the shore, the points extending out almost to the main pack. Through this ice, or rather land water, of the width of $1\frac{1}{2}$ mile, we threaded our way in the darkness, the white glare of the pack on the one hand, and the gleam of the snow-clad land on the other, being our only guides; compass we had none, and once only during the night a solitary star shone out for about ten minutes, giving the helmsman a direction for steering. We were on several occasions so close to the land that I thought we must go ashore, as we had really no guide during the snow squalls, and in the intervals we were frequently obliged to steer by the land astern, and it was somewhat ridiculous to see the helmsman facing aft at the wheel. As the wind increased, and came over the pack, the temperature fell to 18° Fahr., and the spray froze over the ship. By midnight our decks were full of snow, which whirled up in blinding drifts, from the eddy round the sails.

We could from time to time judge our position along the coast by the excellent descriptions by Sir James Ross and M'Clintock of their winter journey. Thus, at 9 P.M., we passed a deep fissure or gorge, separating the limestone from the red sandstone, and which we had noticed when passing the previous week. We continued on, the wind and snow increasing, and the pack evidently closing in, until 3 A.M., when we suddenly observed the ice to trend north and south right across our path. I immediately hove-about, just clearing the solid floe; at the same time a high, precipitous cliff showed out over us, presenting a most ghastly and horrible appearance, with a fringe of ice at the foot, and the horizontal strata appearing like huge bars of some gigantic iron cage, and perfectly black in contrast with the snowy face. I could only see the summit, the strata, and the foot. It was a skeleton of the land, and we appeared to be right within its grasp. We saw this apparition for a few moments only; running aloft, I saw from the topsail-yard that we were absolutely stopped and hemmed in a pool of water, with no egress, and close under the cliffs, with the pack approaching. In a moment all was darkness again, and having got a pressure of steam, we forced the ship off the land, in the direction of the pack, for it certainly looked as though we were to be driven on shore.

At 5.30 we had good daylight, and I could just distinguish a break in the pack, leading towards the open water N.E. of us, but with a barrier of about 100 yards of ice stopping the way. There was no other chance, and to lose this would have been fatal; so, putting on all steam and sail, we ran at it and charged through, finding that it was not so solid as it at first appeared. We were again in the open sea, and, as I expected, our chief danger ended at Cape Rennell. On getting through we appeared to lose all sight of ice ahead, and suddenly found ourselves in a rolling sea, covered, however, for at least 4 miles with young ice, or rather sludge, which acted like oil on the waters, and was so plastic as to take all the undulations of the sea.

Running on before the gale, we sighted Leopold Island in an interval of clear weather, but lost it again in a few minutes. At eleven we saw a heavy pack of ice to the southeast and east of us, so we hauled out to the northward to clear, and getting under two close-reefed topsails and fore-and-aft canvas, we banked the fires, to give the engineers a rest. The barometer now fell to 29.40, in the continued heavy snowdrift. We hove-to, only being able to see a few yards, and a high sea running, with a fresh gale N.W. Land appeared from Beechey Island, and 20 miles to the east on the north shore, and Leopold Island on the south, and we were evidently in a good position in the middle of the straits.

CHAPTER XII.

SECOND VISIT TO THE CARY ISLANDS.

On September 7 we got out of Lancaster Sound, and passed Cape Horsburgh, having for forty-eight hours been scudding under close-reefed topsails, in a heavy gale from the N.W., with a dense snowdrift, and the barometer down to 29.40. It was 22° Fahr., and bitterly cold, and the waves froze as they washed up our sides. We caught occasional glimpses of the north land, which guided us, for we could scarcely see at any time more than a mile from the ship, and we had neither sun, moon, stars, nor available compass, for the violent rolling of the ship caused our binnacle compasses, with their weak horizontal force, to spin round continually. Anxiously I watched our approach to Cape Bullen, for there, on the 22nd of August, we saw that the pack, which arrested us off Cape Warrender, extended quite across the straits. We then calculated that at least 50 miles east and west were entirely blocked, and it was only by working through narrow leads into the shore and the mouth of Admiralty Inlet that we succeeded in getting through. Now all was clear water, and by 9 P.M. on the 6th we had approached Cape Warrender, finding ourselves about half a mile from the glacier, a little to the west end of the cape, and saw some heavy pieces of ice and many bergs, apparently aground, and experienced also a strong current running to the westward, causing the sea to break in a formidable manner, and in the gale that was blowing at the time the top of this breaking sea frequently came over our quarters and taffrail.

Curiously enough, in scudding past Cape Bullen, we suddenly observed under the lee bow, or S.E. of us, what appeared to be a pointed rock, about 10 feet above the water, but which proved to be only a piece of earth-stained ice. This bears upon the rocks which appear on the Admiralty Chart in Lancaster Sound, on the authority of Captain Adams, which I do not in the least believe to exist.

The state and appearance of our poor 'Pandora,' as we emerged from Lancaster Sound was very extraordinary. We had been driving under close-reefed sails since escaping from the pack off Cape Rennell, and the sea, which constantly dashed against our sides, freezing as it rose, had covered our ship on the port side with a solid mass of ice from the doubling up to the rail, whilst the bows, from the figure-head to the anchor, were all frozen into a solid mass, and looking over the stern a fringe of enormous icicles hung down to the water's level.

It was now my intention to endeavour to reach the Cary Islands, and possibly Littleton Island, in order if possible to obtain news of the Government ships.

" At Ivitot our sailors bought a pig, which was petted to the last degree, and so jealous were they of his rights that the dogs were driven in all directions that poor Dennis, as they christened the pig, might not be disturbed. The dogs made several attempts to attack this favoured animal, but a constant look-out, such as one could never expect for any ice, rock, or land from any seaman on board, was kept, and the dogs were driven off at the moment when victory seemed certain. Pea-soup, broken biscuits, and slops of all sorts were given to the dainty animal, whereas if a dog attempted to ask for a share of the remains of the sailors' dinners he was scouted with derision. In fact, the pig was the pet of the ship, and the only thing worth navigating the Arctic Seas for. Finding that he was uncomfortable under

F

the topgallant forecastle, and liable to be disturbed by the
chain running out when anchoring, or the water coming in at
the hawse-pipe when at sea, a snug cask was found for him,
and he was housed in with canvas and straw under the bows
of the long-boat.   Never, I should think, had any other pig
such comforts showered on him.   But now came a change.
Our decks became full of snow, and everything froze.   It was
necessary to clean away the ice and dirt from Mr. Pig's sty
as well as from the other parts of the ship, and to do this involved an amount of scraping which was not agreeable to his
former friends, and with the decision and readiness in meeting
difficulties for which the British seaman is so pre-eminent,
the pig was condemned to death without remorse or apology.
In fact, from that moment he was a nuisance, and only fit to
be killed and eaten: his throat was cut by his dearest friends,
and he was eaten (September 7) for dinner, having died only
at 10 A.M.   Such are the caprices of the true British tar; but
I must add that Mr. Pig's former owner sent an excellent
joint to the wardroom, which was much appreciated."

(Sept. 8–9.) We continued in our effort to reach the
Cary Islands, to ascertain if by chance the 'Alert' and
'Discovery' could possibly have called there after our leaving their letters on the 18th ultimo.   I considered that after
the 10th of this month the navigation of these seas would
become a race against time, but I was not prepared for the
violent N.N.W. gale which we had experienced during the
last forty-eight hours.   It had blown without ceasing, with a
high breaking sea, and the spray drifting across the ship
had frozen over all.   We were one mass of ice.   Our bow-
sprit, figure-head, and anchors were all cemented together,
and both sides, from the water-line to the rail, were covered
with a shield of ice 2 inches thick.   On deck we had a mix-
ture of sludge, ice, and snow, which required the whole
attention of the watch to clear off.   We had been standing to

the N.E. and E.N.E. under close-reefed canvas, not having used our steam since passing Cape Rennell. The sea ran up in great heaps, and occasionally broke on board, and our prospect of getting northward appeared hopeless until this evening, when the gale moderated, and we got up steam, and proceeded towards the Cary Islands, which were about 45 miles distant. At dusk we could just see Wolstenholme Island to the N.E., appearing like an elongated cone, and as a white shadow in the distance. We saw no signs of life, save a few mullemokkes, who shared the discomforts of the gale with us, and followed in our wake. The barometer, which had fallen to 29.40, was now rising, and the sea going down. I resolved to try to land on the island, and re-examine the cairn; but if this proved impracticable I determined to bear up for England, as nothing more could be done that season. The temperature averaged 23° to 18° Fahr. during the last forty-eight hours. It snowed nearly all night, but cleared over the eastern land about 6 A.M. I could distinguish Wolstenholme Island in the E.S.E., and the land about Cape Parry and Booth Sound in the N.E.

(Sept. 10.) To seaward all was dark. We were surrounded with icebergs of every conceivable size and shape, and the late gales appeared to have made great havoc amongst them, there being quantities of broken pieces in the water. Passing through one of these patches of broken ice, I took the opportunity to get a quantity on board, as we were quite out of fresh water, the last, which we pumped in from the floe, having proved to be brackish. Feeling confident of our position, and that we were close to the Cary Islands, although we could not see a mile to the westward, I hove-to until 9 A.M., when, the mist having lifted, I could see the S.E. Cary Island, distant about 3 miles, bearing N.W. Having determined to search all the islands of the group, so that there could be no chance of missing Captain Nares' record, if he had left one, I stood close alongside the S.E. island, and in passing saw a cairn. I did not at first attach much importance to this discovery, Captain Nares having said that his record would be on the N.W. island; but having so thoroughly searched the latter in August, I determined, if the weather permitted, to go through the entire group. Having rounded-to close under the northern side of the island, I dispatched a boat's crew, in charge of Lillingston, Beynan, and Toms, to examine the cairn. They landed with some difficulty, ascended through the deep snow to a height of 650 feet, and hastening on board, delivered to me the record case, containing letters, and an account of the proceedings of the 'Alert' and 'Discovery.' We were thus rewarded for all the hard work of the last few days, and for the risk in proceeding northward at this late season; and we had the satisfaction of bringing home news of the Government ships, which would be most welcome to the public and to the friends of all the members of the expedition.[1] Had we not returned this winter, or gone home with a report that nothing was known of the ships at these islands, considerable anxiety would probably have been felt. It was,

---

[1] The Arctic Expedition, as has been stated already, sailed from Upernivik at 8 A.M. on the 22nd of July, 1875, and shaped a course due west, intending to make a dash through the middle pack instead of creeping round the land ice in Melville Bay. At 1 A.M. on the 23rd the pack edge was sighted, and the two vessels were at once pushed into it. The ice was very loose, not more than 12 inches thick, and with lanes of water in all directions. At 11 A.M. on Sunday, the 25th of July, the 'Alert' and 'Discovery' got clear of the pack and entered the "North Water" of Baffin's Bay, having been only thirty-four hours in the ice, and seventy hours in going from Upernivik to Cape York.

The 'Discovery' then went inshore to communicate with the natives at Cape York, and endeavour to engage a brother-in-law of Hans as second dog-driver. The 'Alert' proceeded to the Cary group, and reached the S.E. island at midnight on the 26th of July. Records and letters, as well as the depôt and a boat, were landed, and a cairn erected. The expedition then proceeded to Smith Sound, with the brightest prospect of an open sea, and of being able to reach a high northern latitude in the season of 1875.

however, by the merest chance that the cairn was seen, as I little expected to find anything on the S.E. island.

A notice was left in Captain Nares' cairn to the effect that we had removed his record and the letters for England, and explaining our second visit to the Cary Islands, and where he would find the letters which we deposited on the N.W. island in August.

The boat only just returned in time, for almost before she was hoisted up, a blinding snowstorm came up from the southward, during which we could not see a cable's length from the ship. Such are the dangers of cruising in these seas at this late season; it is absolutely unsafe to send a boat away unless the ship is securely anchored; the changes are so sudden and severe that it is impossible to depend upon landing upon any exposed shore, or on again reaching the ship. I was only too thankful to see my boat's crew safely on board again on so awful a day.

CHAPTER XIII.

THE VOYAGE HOME.

THE next day (Sept. 11) the sky cleared and the wind backed round to the N.W., and continued all day light with fine clear weather. We were now steering towards the S.E., and by night saw Cape Dudley Digges about 10 miles distant; the wind freshening to a gale, with a high following sea, which froze as it lapped our sides.

Shortly after midnight (Sept. 12) we passed through a quantity of ice lying off Cape York, having previously gone through a complete chain of bergs, apparently aground, and reaching out from the land about the conical rock to 20 miles seaward in a S.W. direction. The storm was too heavy to think of sounding. I felt that we were going over a bank, but the size of the bergs was quite sufficient evidence that we had plenty of water, although the sea broke heavily over our quarters. It is curious how this ice appears to hang about Cape York, and I cannot help thinking that there must be N.W. an eddy current setting round out of Melville Bay, constantly bringing up the ice which hangs about the glaciers and the land there, to the vicinity of Cape York; otherwise, in such a gale as we had experienced, it must soon have scattered to the S.E. By 4 A.M. it was almost daylight, and we were greatly relieved on finding that no ice was visible to the south or S.W., save a few large bergs. The gale diminished towards evening, and by six o'clock, after Divine Service, we got up steam and proceeded slowly through the night, with light variable winds. At noon this day our position by observation was 75° 2′ N., 65° 25′ W   Temperature 24° to 25° Fahrenheit.

The barometer rose (Sept. 13) and we had overcast weather with light east and S.E. winds. We had made, since yesterday, about 78 miles in a S.S.E. direction ; and by noon could just distinguish the land about Wilcox Head and the Devil's Thumb. A high swell commenced from the southward, followed by a gale from the S.E. by E. to S.E., compelling us to heave-to under low sail. The night was intensely dark, sleet fell in showers, and everything seemed damp and miserable. We could only hope that we were well off the middle ice. The ship plunged bows under, but was quite buoyant and lively since having been lightened of her coals.

On the 14th and 15th we had a whole gale from S.E. with thick weather and constant sleet and snow, and a very high sea rolling up from south (true). We saw no ice save here and there a solitary berg, and lay-to under reefed topsails, occasionally to keep our position. On the 15th we saw an enormous berg, which, from its length, I at first mistook for Horse's Head. It was at least a mile long, and through the mist and gloom appeared still larger.

On the 16th the wind came round to the northward, and we progressed south, being at noon in lat. 72° 49′ N., long. 59° 4′ W., and next day sighted the land about the Svarte Huk. About lat. 71° 31′, long. 57° 6′, we passed an immense number of large bergs, but we had not seen a piece of floe ice since leaving Cape York, and I incline to the opinion that with a good ship, properly equipped and rigged to encounter bad weather, and the crew clothed for extreme variations of temperature, this would be the best month to make a passage northward through Melville Bay.

On the night of the 17th we had the first rain since entering Melville Bay on the 15th August. The moon, which had shone so clearly for the last two nights, was quite obscured; and I consequently reduced sail, so as to have the ship under easy command in case of having to clear the icebergs or the land.

(Sept. 20.) On the 19th we arrived off the harbour of Godhavn, having had variable strong winds since the 17th, and having run close along the west side of Disco with a N.E. gale until 8 P.M., when it fell calm. We came close past Fortune Bay and the off-lying islands and rocks, under steam; and when off the entrance to Godhavn we fired a gun, which was soon answered by a light on shore, and we anchored at 3 A.M. After passing Svarte Huk, we saw and cleared a great many icebergs, which had possibly come out of Omenak Fiord. Several were also lying under the land of Disco, and in the entrance to Disco Fiord and Laxe Bay.

(Sept. 24.) We sailed out of Godhaven, having been at anchor four days, and not being able to leave earlier owing to a constant strong south-east wind, with torrents of rain and snow all the time. On the 21st, Lillingston and Pirie went round to Disco Fiord in the steam-cutter, returning all right, much to my relief, on the night of the 22nd, thoroughly drenched, and having had some difficulty in getting round, owing to the heavy sea outside. They had camped one night in the boat in the fiord, and brought back some ducks which they had shot. During our stay we filled up with water, and took in all our boats except the two whalers, and otherwise prepared for our homeward voyage. The crew had leave on shore every evening until 10 P.M., and the dance-house was open and the usual Eskimo ball kept up with great spirit until that hour. The Greenlanders here appear to have been quite spoilt by the number of ships which have recently visited this port, begged incessantly for tobacco or rum, and tried to impose upon our crew by offering them the most useless articles for barter. On entering the port, a boat rope was missing, and not being returned by the pilot's boat crew as promised, I refused all admission to the ship, and was sorry also to have to deny the pilot his privilege of taking the vessel out, whereby he lost the usual present, and appeared much disappointed on my telling him that I did not require his services.

The winds were principally from the north and east, occasionally freshening to a moderate gale, for the first five days of our homeward voyage. Our propeller was lifted, and we were fairly under canvas, having had our fires lighted up to the 25th inst., fifty-nine consecutive days, and still having 45 tons of the best Welsh coal. We passed one or two icebergs, which appeared much broken by the sea, and although the nights had been intensely dark, we had had no occasion for any anxiety, as the seas had been almost free since leaving S.E. Bay and in the meridian of 55° which we had kept to. The barometer had been very low for the last twenty-four hours, 29.20 with overcast sky, and we had now baffling winds, with a tremendous and confused sea, principally from the S.E. (*true*), and I supposed that a heavy gale was blowing round the land from that direction, especially as numbers of mullemokkes were gathered around the ship. We were under close reefs, the ship rolling and pitching in such a manner as to make things thoroughly uncomfortable.

(Sept. 30.) The high confused sea continued all night and throughout the next day, and I felt certain that a heavy gale had been blowing from the south-eastward, round the Cape, and that we were experiencing the eddy winds and back sea. Towards evening the wind became more steady from the N.N.W., but there was still the heavy pyramidal sea, which caused the ship to tumble in such a manner as to render it impossible to walk about. Hundreds of mullemokkes flew around, and I observed a piece of drift pine about

15 feet long and 6 in diameter. We lost two topgallant yards and a jibboom, and were busy to-day making a new maintopsail yard. The barometer rose to 29.30, and the temperature to 42 Fahr.

On October 1st we had most brilliant displays of aurora, after which came frequent snow showers, ending in a brilliant morning. At noon we were to the southward of the Cape, and steering direct for the English Channel, Bishop's Light, Scilly, being 1651 miles distant, bearing S. 70° E.

We had most brilliant weather until the 4th, with moderate breezes from the northward, but the magnificent auroras which every evening lighted up the heavens almost as brightly as the full moon, together with a rapidly falling barometer and a confused sea, all prepared us for the heavy gale which soon burst upon us, in lat. 57° 11′ N., long. 46° 3′ W. The wind commenced from about north, with heavy clouds full of rain, and then gradually backed to the N.N.W., when it blew with the utmost fury. I expected every minute that something would give out, or our canvas burst. A high breaking sea came up on the quarter, but by altering our course according to the change in the direction of the wind, we escaped being boarded by heavy water, although floods of spray came across us. The wind then settled down into a steady fresh gale from the W.N.W., and we scudded before it to the E.S.E., the barometer rising from 29.20 to 29.90, and the sea becoming more regular and true to the wind. We were in lat. 55° 54′, long. 42° 44′ W. at noon by observation, Scilly bearing S. 75° E. 1357 miles.

In the evening of the 5th, soon after eight o'clock, we had another brilliant display of aurora, which lighted up the sky and sea in a manner which I never before witnessed. It appeared first in the W.N.W., in luminous patches, at an elevation of 30 degrees, and quickly ascended towards the zenith, and almost immediately other corruscations shot up from the northward, extending across the zenith to S.S.W., and forming into vertical bands, having that peculiar serpentine motion so well known to Arctic voyagers. The reflection upon the crests of the seas was most beautiful, and as we scudded before the gale we could distinguish each break of the waves for miles astern of the ship. By nine o'clock the lights had quite disappeared, and high threatening clouds, arising in the westward, gave promise of a wild night. The barometer had risen all day, and it had been observed in running down Davis Straits that the mercury invariably fell with an approaching northward gale, being followed by a corresponding rise when the wind backed into the S.W. and southward.

A storm commenced on the evening of the 6th, so suddenly that we had barely time to reduce the canvas. It blew through the night, with torrents of rain and violent squalls, from W.S.W. until morning, when it backed into the W.N.W., and increased until I thought that the close-reefed topsails under which we scudded must give out. We had frequent squalls of hail, and the sea increased to so awful a height that I feared we could not run any longer.

During the night of the 8th the sky presented the most terrific appearance; dense masses of clouds, apparently stationary, surrounded us like a wall, their upper edges illuminated with a brilliant aurora, making their centres and lower strata appear correspondingly black, and out of these black dense masses, a sudden gleam of lightning would occasionally flash, like the flame from the muzzle of a gun, followed quickly by terrific blasts of wind and hail. The storm blew with hurricane force, still increasing, all the forenoon of the 9th; we battened everything down, and as it was not now possible to heave-to, I trusted to scudding before it, which we did all the forenoon, with heavy sea coming over both sides, and one over the stern, filling the deck fore and aft. I never saw so frightful a sea excepting in a typhoon or cyclone, and could not have believed that so violent a storm ever blew in extra-tropical latitudes. The barometer oscillated rapidly, sometimes rising above 30°, but never going below 29.20, and I was consequently little prepared for such a scene. However, we fortunately got through it, by extreme care in steering the ship, and without damage beyond the smashing of a boat. The storm abated about 4 P.M. on the 8th, the wind continuing through the night with occasional squalls from the westward, and the sea subsiding. The wind then backed into the S.W., blowing fresh, with rain, and a continuous gale from the westward for the next two days, before which we scudded under close reefs, and battened down. On the 11th the storm again increased, with violent squalls and tremendous sea, and we carried all sail possible, being frequently deluged with water. At noon we passed two barques, lying-to with nothing but lower maintopsail set. The barometer fell from 29.90 to 29.70, where it remained all day, and this was the only indication we had of the terrible gale we were experiencing. On the 11th the gale moderated, and settled down to a strong N.W. wind, the sea causing the ship to lurch heavily throughout the night. On the 12th two ships were in sight, steering to the eastward under very low sail, and in the evening we passed a small topsail schooner standing to the northward. We were now in lat. 49° 26′ N., long. 10° 12′ W., the Bishop's Light being N. 80°, E. 167 miles. In the evening the wind backed into the southward with torrents of rain and barometer falling rapidly. On the 13th we lost our jibboom, and it was with some difficulty that we got the sail stowed, owing to the weight of water in it. The barometer at midnight was down to 28.90, and the wind suddenly backed into the westward until 3 A.M., when it as suddenly flew into the northward and N.N.E. to N.E., and blew with almost hurricane force.

We entered the Channel on the 14th, making all sail at daylight, the morning being quite fine, but the sky looked threatening, heavy banks of clouds hanging to the northward, with occasional flashes of lightning. The wind was north to N.N.E., and we hauled up towards the English coast as well as we were able. In the afternoon a gale from the northward arose so suddenly that we had barely time to reduce to close reefs. We sent down topgallant yards and got the funnel up and screw down, and lighted the fires. We steered by the wind, making about E. by N., with a strong gale north, a breaking sea, and barometer 29.40 to 29.35. On the night of the 14th we had a heavy gale N.N.E., and carried close-reefed topsails until 4 A.M., when we stowed them, and proceeded under steam and fore-and-aft canvas, making about an east course, and a very heavy breaking sea throughout the morning. At six we sighted the Caskets, and shortly afterwards Alderney, and stood on till ten, when we tacked to northward, and again at noon to the eastward, the sea going down and weather improving. By 6 P.M. we had Alderney dipping, and bearing S. by W. We made but slow progress towards the Wight, and were tantalized by seeing the 'Alice,' Jersey steamer, dash past us at 10 miles an hour.

On the 16th we anchored at Spithead.

APPENDIX.

APPENDIX.

———◆◇◆———

A.

LETTER from ADMIRAL RICHARDS to the *Times*, dated Oct. 23, 1875, enclosing EXTRACTS of a LETTER from COMMANDER MARKHAM, of H.M.S. 'ALERT.'

To the Editor of the Times.

"SIR,—When the 'Pandora' left Portsmouth in June last, the object of her voyage was to a great extent shrouded in mystery. Little more could be gathered than that she was provisioned and equipped to pass a winter in the ice, and that she was receiving letters for the Polar Expedition which had preceded her a month.

"It was known, of course, that Captain Allen Young was an experienced Arctic navigator, that he had some able naval and other officers under his command, and that he was accompanied by a staff of talented correspondents, naturalists, artists, &c., with a small but picked crew equal to any service they might be called on to perform. Under these circumstances, and without any display, he quietly sailed out of Portsmouth Harbour on the 20th June last for the Arctic Regions.

"But Captain Young's aims were not purposeless, and he did not leave England without confiding to a few of his Arctic friends what his hopes and intentions were. I confess I was among those who believed that he displayed a wise discretion in his reticence.

"The 'Pandora' has returned, probably, before many expected her, and though the incidents of her voyage have been ably and graphically depicted by the talented special correspondent, it has not appeared very clearly or authoritatively what were the precise objects of her cruise, or why she returned. A few words in your columns, therefore, from one who has no personal interest in the matter, and who does not overstep the bounds of confidence in writing them, may not be unfitting at the present time.

"It is generally known that the late Lady Franklin entertained to the end of her life an unalterable conviction that some records of her husband's expedition still lay buried on King William's Land, off the shores of which his ships were abandoned in 1848. However much Arctic authorities may have differed as to the utility of a further search for those documents, Captain Allen Young was always anxious to gratify this natural desire, and, indeed, was the only one interested in the subject whose private means would permit him to do so.

"More than once he went so far as to purchase a vessel with the view of carrying out this object, though from one cause or another his efforts were frustrated. Last year, however, he succeeded in obtaining a suitable vessel in the 'Pandora,' and with the assistance of one or two associates who joined him in the enterprise, he strengthened and completely equipped her for Arctic service, himself assuming the command; and although he was probably encouraged by the change which had been gradually coming over public opinion in regard to Polar exploration, and by the decision of the Government to send out an expedition, it is pretty certain that he would have carried out his favourite project irrespective of either of these considerations.

"The 'Pandora' then left England and passed by the usual route through Davis's Strait and Lancaster Sound, but instead of sailing down Prince Regent Inlet and trying Bellot Strait, where M'Clintock had been arrested in the 'Fox,' Captain Young pushed down Peel Sound to the westward, which had scarcely before been attempted by ship, but which was very generally believed to be the true gateway to the North-West Passage along the coast of America, which Collinson, in the 'Enterprise,' so nearly effected from Behring Strait.

"Could the 'Pandora' have passed the barrier of ice which choked the narrow throat of this sound about 120 miles within its entrance, and the northern edge of which she reached, there is little doubt in my mind that Captain Young would have accomplished the North-West Passage, and he would at the same time have had an opportunity of re-examining the western shores of King William's Land under favourable circumstances, but when he had reached this barrier, and saw from an eminence the western entrance of Bellot Strait, with firm ice stretching right across Peel

Sound, he saw that there was little or no hope of effecting the passage during the present season. It was manifest then that he must either return or adopt the alternative course of seeking winter quarters, the nearest shelter being 40 miles to the northward. In the latter case the 'Pandora' would not have been advantageously placed for travelling as the 'Fox' was under M'Clintock, when he discovered the fate of Franklin, and all that could have been done would have been in the summer of 1876, to have re-examined, under less favourable circumstances, a portion of the ground traversed by M'Clintock, Hobson, and himself fifteen years before. It must be admitted, then, I think, that a sound judgment was exercised in the course which was adopted.

"But if Captain Young failed to accomplish with his little vessel what has never yet been achieved with greater means—viz. the passing by ship from one ocean to another—he has rendered good service to the Government expedition, which deserves to be recorded.

"The last intelligence received from the 'Alert' and 'Discovery' was dated from Disco, the 17th of July, and we had no reason to expect anything further, unless from Upernivik—a short distance to the north—until their return in 1876 or 1877. Now, from Disco to the entrance of Smith Sound, a distance of about 600 miles, is the most difficult and critical portion of an outward Polar voyage, and through Captain Young's perseverance we now know that the ships arrived safely at the Cary Islands, within 100 miles of Smith Sound, after a remarkably successful run of nine days from Disco, including stoppages. It is true that Captain Young had promised the Commander of the Polar Expedition that he would endeavour to communicate with the Cary Isles, but the chances against his being able to do so were considerable, and were perfectly understood to be so by Captain Nares. Not only did Captain Young go considerably out of his way to fulfil his promise on his outward voyage, when he was late in the season and had an important object of his own in view in another direction, but failing then to find the records, he made a second attempt late in the year, when his own enterprise was at an end, and against a heavy northerly gale and very severe weather, again fetched the Cary Isles on the 10th of September, and discovered and brought away the intelligence which must have been alike satisfactory to

G

the Government and comforting to all who have friends in the expedition.

" From this information we learn that the ships left Upernivik, the northernmost Danish port in Greenland, on the 22nd of July, and that Captain Nares, by boldly pushing out into the middle ice, had achieved in five days what formerly occupied more than as many weeks to accomplish, with harassing labour, in sailing vessels, along the land ice of Melville Bay. In a short note to myself from Cary Isles, dated July 27th, Captain Nares describes the season as most favourable, and their prospects bright beyond anything they could have hoped for; and an extract from a private letter which has been put at my disposal, and which you may, perhaps, think will be of interest to your readers, speaks also more hopefully of their prospects. It is from Commander Markham, of the 'Alert.' No doubt the season has been favourable, but I am inclined to believe that unfavourable seasons were more impressed upon us formerly from the absence of steam-power.

" There can be no question but that the prospect from the Cary Isles was very promising. Northerly winds and a current of a mile and a half an hour had apparently cleared out the ice to the north, and no doubt existed in Captain Nares's mind but that they would be within the Sound in less than two days. This fair prospect was corroborated by Captain Young, who observed the same favourable state of things on the 18th of August, and again on the 10th of September.

" Humanly speaking, therefore, the programme, so far as it could be laid down with any degree of certainty, has probably been accomplished; and less than 300 miles from the entrance of Smith Sound would place the 'Discovery' in the position hoped for. What lies beyond the 82nd parallel we must wait to learn; in the meantime there is much cause for hope and confidence. Most people will probably agree that Captain Young has more than fulfilled his promise—a promise spontaneously and generously made, and carried out at some sacrifice.

" The 'Pandora' would gladly have followed the Polar explorers on the 10th of September, tempestuous, though promising, as the prospect was then to her; but those who know Captain Allen Young will best understand the delicacy which forbade him to seek a share of the honours where he could not add to the resources, and where possible disaster might have caused him and his gallant companions to become an extra burden upon them.

"I am, Sir,

"Your obedient servant,

"GEO. HENRY RICHARDS, *Rear-Admiral.*

"ATHENÆUM CLUB, *Oct.* 23."

EXTRACTS of a LETTER from COMMANDER A. H. MARKHAM, of H.M.S. 'ALERT,' referred to by ADMIRAL RICHARDS:—

"*Friday, July* 23, *off Cape Shackleton.*—We are now steaming full speed, being beautiful calm weather, towards the westward to make the pack edge, which we shall probably do in three hours' time. We have had a very busy day to-day. In the first place, at six o'clock this morning, the fog being too thick to proceed, we endeavoured to get into a little bay on the island of Kingitok, to anchor and wait for clear weather. In doing so we ran on a rock, and remained immoveable for five hours. No damage, however, was done. The ice-saw crews have been organized, and officers and men appointed to the different boats in case of having to abandon the ship. Everything has been prepared for lifting the screw and rudder, and altogether we have had a busy day. Our knapsacks are all packed ready for leaving the ship. I am quite surprised at the amount of water. We have as yet seen no pack ice whatever. I do really believe we are going to have a remarkably open season, and that we shall get as far north as our most sanguine expectations can suggest.

"*Saturday, July* 24.—We have been so far wonderfully lucky, and are all much elated at the prospect of success before us. We made the pack edge about two o'clock this morning, and pushed into it, since which time we have been steaming through. The ice is wonderfully open, and we have hitherto gone on without the slightest check. There are lanes of water in all directions, and if the weather will only remain fine and calm we shall in all probability get into the 'North Water' to-morrow. The ice is by no means heavy, the greater part of it only about 12 inches thick, by which I think it is this spring's formation. If we only have to encounter ice of the same thickness in Smith Sound, we shall be able to steam straight up to the North Pole this year. At present everything points to speedy success; but a few hours make a wonderful difference in these regions. We must hope for the best. If we go on at the rate we have been going to-day, we shall get to the Cary Islands on Tuesday.

"*Sunday, July* 25.—We have had unparalleled success, and are actually in the 'North Water,' passing Cape York. I believe our passage is almost unprecedented. We only entered the ice of the middle pack at two o'clock yesterday morning, and at eleven this forenoon, just thirty-four hours in the ice, we emerged in the 'North Water.' Including stoppages, we have only been seventy hours going from Upernivik to Cape York. We certainly have been most fortunate in our weather—not a breath of wind since we made the pack, which was so loose as to render navigation through it a matter of ease. Everything appears favourable to the northward. Little ice can be seen, and all seems clear and open. We parted company with the 'Discovery' at six o'clock this evening. She has gone in towards Cape York to communicate with the natives, and induce one of them, a brother-in-law of Hans, to join as dog-driver. We are now steering along the Crimson Cliffs of Beverley, with Cape Dudley Digges ahead, on our way to the Cary Islands, where we shall establish our first depôt, and land our letters for Allen Young to pick up. Having completed our work, we shall go to Littleton Island, and join the 'Discovery' either there or at Sutherland Island. I am afraid the 'Discovery' will not be able to send any letters, as they have not sent any to us, and will not visit the Cary Islands.

"*Monday, July* 26.—A dense fog came on this morning and lasted all day, so with all the numerous icebergs about, we are obliged to go on carefully. We shall probably get in at ten or twelve o'clock to-night. I have got all the depôt prepared for landing, so it ought not to take us more than six hours putting it on shore and securing it. To-morrow forenoon we ought to be on our way to Littleton Island. Everything is still in our favour. A light breeze from the northward is blowing, which will nicely clear Smith Sound for us. Not a bit of pack ice is to be seen to-day, and the temperature of the water is very high. I believe our success is going to be most complete."

B.

Letters to the ' Times ' from the Rev. G. Haughton and Captain
Allen Young on the Tidal Barrier.

To the Editor of the ' Times.'

" Sir,—In the year 1857, when M'Clintock was about to set out
on his search for Franklin in the ' Fox,' I called his attention to
the probability that there is a permanent tidal ice-barrier all
through the Arctic Archipelago, caused by the still water occa-
sioned by the meeting of the Davis's Strait and Behring's Strait
tides from the Atlantic and Pacific Oceans ; and I ventured at
that time to draw on the chart the most probable line of junction
of the Atlantic and Pacific tides, in the portion of the Archipelago
which he was about to search. The ' Erebus ' and ' Terror ' were
beset and perished within a very short distance of the tidal barrier
line so drawn.

" It is well known from the experience of Collinson and M'Clure
that vessels can enter the Arctic Archipelago through Behring's
Straits and sail to the eastward and north-eastward, to within some
50 or 60 miles of places which can be easily reached from the
Atlantic side through Lancaster Sound.

" The ships from Behring's Strait always find themselves in
the Pacific tide, and the ships from Lancaster Sound always find
themselves in the Atlantic tide, but no ship has yet crossed the
tidal ice-barrier, and passed into the open water of the other ocean,
and I believe no ship ever will do so.

" The recent voyage of the ' Pandora ' is simply a repetition of
the experiment so often made unsuccessfully to cross this barrier.
The ' Pandora ' found no difficulty, having reached Lancaster
Sound, in pushing on to Beechey Island, and afterwards in making
her way down Peel Sound (Franklin Channel), along the very
route traversed by the unfortunate ' Erebus ' and ' Terror,' but as
soon as she had reached La Roquette Island, at the western
entrance of Bellot Strait, she met the ice-barrier 25 feet thick and
50 miles wide. If the ' Pandora ' had ventured into this barrier,
she would have shared the fate of the ' Erebus ' and ' Terror,' but
she would not have made the North-West Passage.

" Before the Alert ' and ' Discovery ' sailed in this year I wrote to Captain Nares, giving him my reasons for thinking that he would find the tidal ice-barrier after passing through Smith Sound at this side of the North Pole, and I instructed several officers of the expedition in a method of telling quickly whether the ships are in the Atlantic tide or in the Pacific tide.

" If my opinion should turn out to be correct, the wisest course the ships could adopt after meeting the tidal ice-barrier would be to keep well to the southward of it, and trust the entire chances of the expedition to sledge travelling, by means of which it would be probably an easy matter to reach the North Pole.

" I am, Sir, yours faithfully,

" SAMUEL HAUGHTON.

" TRINITY COLLEGE, DUBLIN, *Nov.* 1."

To the Editor of the ' Times.'

" SIR,—Will you allow me to make the following remarks upon Professor Haughton's letter in the ' Times' of to-day?

" It is well known that the learned Professor has given great attention to the universal tidal action, and especially to the tidal wave in the Arctic Seas, and there is no one living whose opinions are more valued. I do not think, however, that it was a tidal barrier which arrested the ' Pandora' on her late voyage, but an accumulation of ice, the result of an exceptional season, and the extraordinary prevalence of strong N.W winds, which drove the Polar pack through M'Clintock Channel, impinging it on the Boothian coast, and blocking the southern part of Franklin Channel, and thus prevented the last winter's ice in those straits from breaking up. The N.W. winds would be as much in favour of clearing the way of the Government expedition going north from Baffin's Sea as they were against my prospect of proceeding south from Barrow Strait, and I trust that Captain Nares has this season reached a very high latitude without meeting any tidal ice-barrier in that direction.

" There is no evidence to prove by which route the ' Erebus' and ' Terror' reached the point at which they were finally beset, and in the absence of such proof I consider that, without detracting from the discoveries of that great navigator, Sir John Franklin, the

'Pandora' may fairly claim to be the first ship ever known to have navigated through Peel's Strait to lat. 72.8, at the entrance of Franklin Channel, and thus to have added one more step in the right direction. I yet hope to make another attempt, and even again failing, I shall still hope on that some future navigator more fortunate than myself may prove the North-West Passage to be open for at least a short season in most years.

" I was on my late voyage fully alive to the great risk to which Professor Haughton alludes of entering the pack which we met. But we found it quite impossible to do so, and wherever we attempted it an impenetrable line of ice, without the slightest lane of water, presented itself to our view. And I quite agree with him that it would have been a very false manœuvre to have allowed our ship to be beset in such a position, and thus to have probably ended our voyage in a disaster.

"I am, Sir,

"Your very obedient servant,

" ALLEN YOUNG,

" *Commander Arctic ship ' Pandora.'*

"1, St. James's Street, S.W., *Nov.* 4."

C.

LETTER from SIR LEOPOLD M'CLINTOCK, to MR. GORDON BENNETT, dated Nov. 3, 1875.

" PORTSMOUTH, ENGLAND, *Nov.* 3.

" DEAR SIR,—You call for my ideas upon the subject of Allen Young's recent voyage into Peel Strait, and you call for it as being yourself deeply interested in Arctic exploration and in all matters relating to the practicability of the North-West Passage. I can have no sort of hesitation in complying with your wish.

" Young was with me in the ' Fox ' when we attempted to pass down Peel Strait, in August, 1858. We were stopped by fixed ice after a run down it of only 25 miles. Without wasting time in waiting there we attempted to pass through Bellot Strait, and

although we succeeded in this, yet our further progress was stopped
by fixed ice across its western outlet. You will remember that my
object was to reach King William's Island. From my position, at
this western outlet of Bellot Strait, I could see that all to the
north, as far as the horizon, was covered with unbroken ice, while
all to the south was water, with the exception of the belt of fixed ice,
some three or four miles wide, which so effectually barred my way.

" Subsequent sledging exploration to the Great Fish River, and
all round King William's Island, convinced me that we actually
saw in that narrow barrier of ice the only impediment to our
progress to and beyond King William's Island. It also convinced
me that Franklin's ships passed down Peel Strait, thus proving that
seasons do occur when it is navigable.

" And now, to sum up. We know of one year (Franklin's) when
Peel Strait was navigable ; of another year (M'Clintock's) when it
was not navigable ; and of a third year (Allen Young's) when it was
partially navigable. In my opinion, this strait, together with its
southern continuation, is probably navigable once in four or five
years ; and if a steamer could then make her way through it before
the close of the month of August, she would be able to complete
the passage from the one ocean to the other before the navigable
season was over.

" Here let me refer you to my narrative of the voyage of the
' Fox ' (later edition, pp. 265–7) for my own opinions, as they were
written down at the time.

" Young's attempt to accomplish the North-West Passage was
as bold and skilful a one as was ever made. He persevered, not
only after all hope seemed extinguished, but until further perseverance would have rendered his retreat impossible ; and here
at the most critical moment of his voyage, I consider that he exercised the soundest judgment and discretion in effecting his escape.
Had his attempt been successful he would not only have accomplished the North-West Passage, but would also have achieved
another object which he had in view—namely, that of searching the
shores of King William's Island, at the only season when they are
free from snow, for further relics of Sir John Franklin's expedition, which perished there in 1848.

" But, although baffled in the main objects of his voyage, other
important and useful work remained for him to do, and well he has

done it.   He has brought us intelligence of our Arctic Expedition
of very great interest.   By it we know that they had surmounted
all the difficulties of Baffin's Bay navigation, had crossed the
dreadful Melville Bay with hardly a check, and that as early as
July 26 they were within one hundred miles of Smith Sound,
where their work of exploration was to begin, and that they were
favoured with an unusually good season.

"But for Allen Young, in the 'Pandora,' this good news could
not have reached us for another year at the least.   The country has
been spared a year's doubts and misgivings; and I trust that
Mr. Young has received from official quarters an acknowledgment
commensurate with the great public service he has thus rendered
at so much personal hazard and cost.

"I remain, dear Sir,

"Faithfully yours,

"F. L. M'CLINTOCK."

D.

LETTER from VICE-ADMIRAL SIR RICHARD COLLINSON to
MISS CRACROFT.

"October 12th, 1875.

"MY DEAR MISS CRACROFT,—I enclose Young's letters to M'Clintock, which I received this morning.   He would like to have them
back when you have done with them.

"The outward passage has been so long that I have no doubt
the loss of daylight will prevent them attempting Peel Sound this
season.   It would be madness to winter anywhere in the neighbourhood of Bellot Strait on that side.   I do not believe there is
an indentation either on North Somerset—W. side—or the Prince
of Wales's Island, that the ice does not move in the winter, and it
will not do to expose the 'Pandora' to a second edition of what
the 'Terror' underwent in Hudson's Bay.   The tide will be the
means by which the passage will be made; but the tide must

H

be encountered with the advantage of daylight and a higher temperature.

"I shall not be surprised to see them in England before the end of the month.

"Yours very sincerely,

"R. COLLINSON."

LONDON : PRINTED BY W. CLOWES AND SONS, STAMFORD STREET AND CHARING CROSS.

www.ingramcontent.com/pod-product-compliance
Ingram Content Group UK Ltd.
Pitfield, Milton Keynes, MK11 3LW, UK
UKHW042151280225
455719UK00001B/257